GW00383077

CONTENTS

INTRODUCTION

The domestic cat (*Felis domesticus*) belongs to the family *Felidae* of the order *Carnivora*, and it is one of the smallest members of a very diverse group that includes lions, tigers, cheetahs and the Scottish wildcat (*Felis catus*). The association between human beings and the cat stretches back for thousands of years and is believed to have its origins in Ancient Egyptian civilization. It is known that as the cultivation of the land became established, with the harvesting of crops and storage of grain in granaries, so this attracted large numbers of mice and other rodents that feasted on, and spoiled, the stored food. It is thought that about 5000 BC, the ancestors of the domestic cat were attracted by this abundance of their natural prey and became accustomed to the habitations of human beings in this way.

Over the following years the process of domestication is believed to have begun, so that by 2000 BC the cat had become a valued and revered animal in Ancient Egyptian culture. Cats were worshipped in Ancient Egypt, and two important cat goddesses were Pashat and Bast, although there were a number of lesser ones. It became an offence, punishable by death, to kill a cat, and the animals were believed to possess the power to influence human health and fertility and the success of harvests. Beautiful, richly decorated shrines and temples were dedicated to the cat deities, and cats are prominently represented in Egyptian art and sculpture. When they died, cats were afforded full religious honours, and their bodies were embalmed and mummified and placed in the tombs reserved for their owners.

For many years Egyptian laws did not permit domestic cats to be taken to other countries. As Egyptian influence declined and trade increased, however, their export began and domestic cats had been introduced to Greece by about 1000 BC.

The Romans kept cats for the practical purpose of keeping down vermin but did not afford them any special status or veneration. Cats accompanied the Roman legions on their numerous expeditions and conquests, and it is almost certain that this was the means by which they were introduced into Britain. By similar means of trade, conquest and settlement, the domestic cat gradually became established in most countries and continents throughout the world.

Human attitudes to cats varied according to the culture in which they were placed. In some countries, they were venerated and revered while in others they were somewhat feared and believed to be associated with evil. Superstitions regarding cats were common in mediaeval times in Britain and Europe, particularly the belief that they were the familiars of witches and associated with black magic and the devil. Even so, cats were always tolerated for their ability to catch and deter vermin, and during the Middle Ages, a good 'mouser' cost about a halfpenny.

It is possible that the combination of aloofness and independence, coupled with occasional displays of great affection, which are so much a part of a cat's nature, are the factors that have provoked such strong reactions in people over the centuries. Human beings may have domesticated the cat, but it is very much on the cat's terms. In many instances, a cat seems to choose to live with its people and reserves the right to alter the arrangement, unlike the dog, which is usually submissive and wishing to please. It is this aspect that gives a cat such fascination and has ensured that, as a pet, it is probably more popular now in Western countries than at any time in the past.

POINTS TO CONSIDER BEFORE

ACQUIRING A CAT

It is generally agreed that having a pet cat is a great deal less demanding than owning a dog. A cat does not need to be exercised and can be trained to use a cat flap or other suitable access point, so that it can come and go as it pleases. Alternatively, it can be taught to use a litter tray so that it can be kept permanently indoors if necessary. As long as it is not spoiled by its owner, a cat is usually easy, undemanding and inexpensive to feed. There is a wide variety of high quality, nutritious and well-balanced commercial foods available, and most cats will eat these quite readily. Many people who have a dog want a particular breed, and this can be expensive to buy. With cats, however, the vast majority are 'mongrels' and one can usually be acquired for nothing or at very little cost. (About 5 per cent of pet cats are purebred pedigree animals, which are quite costly to buy.) The majority of cats are clean and fastidious, although tom cats can have the unpleasant habit of spraying urine in the house to mark their territory. It has to be said that in urban areas, cats can cause considerable annoyance because of their habit of digging in gardens in order to relieve themselves.

This is especially infuriating to people who are keen gardeners and who do not themselves own a cat. It is also not uncommon for cats to use a child's garden sandpit as a toilet, if this is left uncovered, and this is obviously unpleasant and poses a health risk. It is therefore part of responsible ownership to train a kitten to use a corner of its own garden or a litter tray in order to prevent it from being a nuisance to others.

Neutered cats (*see* GROOMING AND CARE—Neutering, page 73) are normally fairly quiet (although Siamese cats are an exception to this rule) and hence do not cause the same degree of nuisance as a barking dog. The same is not true, however, of unneutered cats, and the female, in particular, develops a loud, persistent, high-pitched miaow (known as 'calling') when she is in season or oestrous (*see* SEXUAL BEHAVIOUR AND BREEDING—Female Cat, page 94). An unneutered tom cat may also call when he is patrolling his territory to check up on the likelihood of one of the females in the area being ready to mate. The noisy racket that is produced during the mating process usually occurs at night and is highly effective in disrupting human sleep. For this reason, as well as the fact that there are vast numbers of unwanted cats, many of them living in a semi-wild state, pets should be neutered unless they are pedigree animals that are of value for breeding.

It can be reasonably said that the costs of acquiring and keeping a pet cat are modest provided that the animal remains fit and well. If a cat becomes ill or involved in an accident, however, veterinary costs can be very considerable, and this must be taken into account before acquiring any pet. In addition, there are the routine costs of worming and vaccination (*see* GROOMING AND CARE, pages 70–73), which should be regularly attended to throughout the cat's lifetime.

A visit to the waiting room of any veterinary clinic shows that cats are among the most frequent clients. It is wise to take account of this before having a cat as a pet. Insurance policies are available to take away the worry of being faced with a large veterinary bill but, of course, the cost of these can also be quite high, especially over the whole life span of the cat, which is often fifteen or more years.

In common with most breeds of dog, cats have abundant hair that is shed at certain times of the year. The hair adheres to carpets and furnishings, and this may mean that more effort is needed in cleaning and vacuuming than would otherwise be the case. In addition, people who suffer from asthma and eczema are often allergic to cat hair. If any member of the family suffers from either of these conditions, this should be taken into account before acquiring a cat as a pet.

A final problem of pet-owning is what to do with animals when the owner has to go away from home. It may be possible to find a willing friend or neighbour to feed and look after a cat while you are away, so that the animal can remain in its own home. In general, this is easier to achieve with a cat than with a dog, although many cats do not like being left in an empty house. An alternative is to place the cat in a boarding cattery where it will be well looked after while you are away. This is an additional expense that should be taken into account before acquiring a cat as it can be costly if a cattery is to be used on a regular basis.

Choosing a Pet Kitten

In Britain, 95 per cent of pet cats are mongrel or crossbreed animals. It is probably true to say that once they have made the decision to have a cat, most people acquire a kitten from the nearest litter that they hear about in their neighbourhood. They do not spend a lot of time looking at different groups of kittens or weighing up the 'pros' and 'cons' of the various breeds, as is often the case with choosing a dog. In fact, there are many advantages in choosing a kitten from a mother cat that belongs to a good and caring home and family. One can then be sure that both the mother and kittens have received plenty of care, attention and good feeding and are therefore likely to be free of illnesses or infections. The kittens will also almost certainly have been gently and carefully handled and taught to lap milk and feed independently. They will have started to form good relationships with people and will be more likely to settle happily into a new home.

This, of course, applies both to mongrel and pedigree kittens. The main difference, for those seeking a pedigree kitten of a particular breed, is that it is unlikely that there will be one available in the immediate neighbourhood. If the choice is for a pedigree kitten, then planning is almost always necessary. A good place to start is at the local veterinary clinic where advice can be obtained about the various breeds and the location of breeders. In many towns and cities, there are also local cat clubs, which are useful sources of information. If possible, it is a good idea to visit a local cat show or even a large national event such as the National Cat Club Show held at Olympia in London. One is then able to talk to the owners and breeders and arrange to be contacted when a litter of kittens becomes available. Pedigree kittens, especially those showing all the desirable attributes of the breed and with potential as prizewinners, can be expensive to buy and may be in great demand. In any litter of kittens, however, there may be individuals that are considered slightly less than perfect from the showing point of view, and these are usually less costly. They still make highly desirable pets and usually retain the potential to become parents of prizewinning kittens themselves as faults are not likely to be serious ones.

Whether it is a mongrel or pedigree cat, the sex of the kitten is one factor that must be taken into consideration. In one sense, if the kitten is destined to become a family pet, this is almost irrelevant since it is highly desirable that both males and females should be neutered to prevent them from breeding. At the present time in Britain, there is a superabundance of unwanted cats, and towns, cities and rural areas all have their own populations of feral cats making a living as best they can. Each unneutered cat will undoubtedly add many times to the population explosion as, in ordinary circumstances, it is extremely difficult to prevent mating and breeding. Usually, the males in a litter of kittens are the first to find homes as the neutering operation is more straightforward and less expensive than in the females. Neutered males and females make equally delightful pets. Some people may argue that females are somewhat more home-loving and affectionate and males more independent. These differences, if they exist at all, are very slight, and a great deal depends upon the individual nature and temperament of a cat rather than its sex.

It is probably fair to say that when choosing a kitten from a litter most people are governed by emotional factors rather than rational ones, particularly if there are children present. As already stated, as long as the kittens and their mother are in a good and caring home problems are likely to be insignificant, but there are still one or two points to watch out for. The kitten should appear to be alert and healthy, with a shiny, sleek coat that is free from any sign of skin disorder. The eyes should be bright and clear and the ears free from any sign of discharge or material that might indicate the presence of a problem such as ear mites (*see* PARASITES—External Parasites, page 136). There should be no signs of coughing, sneezing or nasal discharge as these could indicate the presence of a serious illness such as cat flu. The kitten should be friendly, happy to come and greet people and to play with its brothers and sisters. It should not appear to be timid in any way as this might indicate problems in relating to people in the future. The kitten should appear to be well nourished and neither too fat nor too thin. A potbellied appearance could indicate the presence of a heavy infestation of roundworms (*see* PARASITES—Internal Parasites, page 129), which can compromise the health of a very young kitten.

If a kitten is being acquired from an animal rescue shelter then great care is needed to avoid possible disappointment and upset. Sadly, it is often the case that such kittens have been separated from their mother at a very young age, are poorly nourished and have very little resistance to diseases and infections. In fact, it is not uncommon for a kitten to be harbouring a disease that may not manifest itself until after the animal has gone to a new home. It is certainly a much needed and kindly act to offer a home to a kitten like this, but it is wise to recognize that there are potential pitfalls. If it is decided to go ahead, it is sensible to have the kitten checked by a veterinary surgeon so that the best possible advice can be obtained and any health problems treated at an early stage.

One final point to remember is that unless one has a great deal of spare time it is best not to choose the very long-haired types or breeds of cat. These cats require a great deal of grooming to prevent the fur from becoming tangled and knotted into impossible, matted lumps that have to be cut away, sometimes under general anaesthetic (*see* A-Z OF ILLNESSES, INJURIES AND VETERINARY PROCEDURES, page 149).

Choosing an Adult Cat

Because of the problem of the explosion in the cat population, there are many animal rescue centres all over Britain caring for unwanted stray animals. Many of these strays are adult cats that have been living rough or have been abandoned for one reason or another. Animal rescue centres are always keen to find good and caring homes for the cats in their charge as, sadly, there are usually new animals arriving every day and therefore pressure on the spaces available. Generally, the people running the centre try to get to know the cats in their care so that they are able to match a suitable animal with a prospective owner. It is not uncommon to see advertisements in a local paper, which, as well as giving general information about the rescue centre, publish names, descriptions and even photographs of individual cats in the hope of finding good homes for them. Sometimes, if it is felt that a cat is too wary and shy to become a house pet, all that is asked for is a warm and secure bed in an outhouse and a supply of good food. Given time, kindness and patience, even a distrustful cat that has had unhappy experiences at the hands of people may respond and become an affectionate pet. It has to be said, however, that some cats never get over their early bad experiences and always keep their distance, no matter what people try to do.

It can be seen from this that there is certainly no difficulty in acquiring an adult cat in need of a good home, and this is an act of kindness that helps to reduce the vast numbers of unwanted animals. The arrangement often works out very well indeed, both for the cat and its new owners, once the period of adjustment and settling in is past, and this is obviously the best possible outcome. There can, however, be problems with an adult cat, often relating to behaviour patterns that have become ingrained or perhaps to cleanliness, and these may take some time and a great deal of patience to overcome. (*See* Taking Home an Adult Cat, page 30.)

When choosing an adult cat, as in the choice of a kitten, it is important to check as far as possible that the animal is healthy by looking at its general appearance and behaviour, coat, eyes, nose and ears. A cat is likely to have already had a health check and some veterinary care on admittance to a rescue centre and to have been assessed by the staff and will not knowingly be offered for placement if it has an illness.

Once the cat has settled into its new home, however, it may

be advisable to have it checked by a veterinary surgeon, who may well advise a course of vaccination against certain feline illnesses. This is a wise precaution since, if the cat has previously been a stray, it is unlikely to have received any such protection. At the same time, the veterinary surgeon will be able to advise about worming the cat or answer any other queries that the new owners may have. Of course, if more is known about the background of a particular cat, for instance one that is acquired from a relative or friend and has come from a good home, then these precautions are less likely to be necessary.

The Cat that Chooses You

It is sometimes the case that people do not choose to be cat owners but are themselves chosen by the feline in question. A cat can be quite good at turning up on the doorstep, often late at night and in miserable weather, and yowl to be allowed in. If the members of the household give in, as they often do, usually managing at the very least to find a bowl of milk, something to eat and a warm place for the cat to spend the night, this can be the start of the adoption process. The cat may appear to be well nourished and evidently used to being a pet, but advertisements may still fail to find its true owners. The business of advertising and trying to find the former owners is likely to take some days, stretching into weeks and, by then, the people and the cat have often become mutually fond of each other. The cat has found a new home! There are probably a number of different reasons why cats stray away from good and caring homes, but the 'lost and found' columns of newspapers provide evidence that some of them do so.

Sometimes the cat that turns up in the garden or neighbourhood appears much more like a stray, looking thin, ragged and uncared for. Kindly people may start out by just putting out food and drink for the cat and perhaps leaving a shed or garage door open so that it can find some shelter. Depending upon the temperament of the cat, this state of affairs may continue or the animal may adopt winning ways and eventually end up as a house pet.

In both these circumstances, the people involved must decide what they wish to do. If you start feeding and looking after a stray cat, both it and your neighbours are soon likely to regard it as being yours. If you are sure that you do not want a cat, it is best to telephone one of the animal welfare organizations, such as the RSPCA or SSPCA (in Scotland), or a local rescue shelter, and arrange for the animal to be picked up. It is probably best to do this at an early stage, especially if there are children in the home who are likely to want to keep the cat. It is certain that the cat will be well looked after and every effort will be made to find it a good home. No one should take on a cat that has presented itself in this way unless it is a unanimous decision taken by all the members of the household.

Bringing Home a New Kitten

A kitten may be chosen at an earlier stage but, ideally, it should not be taken to its new home until it is about eight weeks of age. This is not a hard-and-fast rule, however, and a kitten may be had at a younger age (from five weeks onwards) as long as it has been taught to lap milk and feed independently on solid food. Much depends upon the number of kittens in a litter. If it is a large litter (six or seven), the kittens are likely to be less advanced at a comparable age than those from a small litter. Obviously, a younger, smaller kitten will require even more special care when it arrives in its new home to ensure that it will thrive.

One or two preparations should be made before the kitten is brought home. A supply of food is, of course, needed. It is best, at first, to find out what the kitten has been used to eating and to buy a supply of the same kind of food. This is one factor that can then remain constant in the kitten's life in the bewildering business of leaving its familiar surroundings and entering a new home. Familiar food is likely to prove reassuring to the kitten, encouraging it to eat and helping with the settling-in process. Two suitable bowls or containers are required, one for food and the other for fluids. Old saucers have often been used for the purpose in the past and are quite suitable. Some people prefer, however, to purchase the shallow, plastic feeding bowls that are on sale in pet shops, and these have the advantage of being nonbreakable and should therefore last for the whole lifetime of the cat.

A suitable container is needed that can be used as a litter tray. There may be something suitable in the home, garage or garden shed, but many people prefer to purchase a litter tray from a pet shop. This is a rectangular-shaped shallow box, usually about 6½ centimetres deep, 30 centimetres long and 20 centimetres wide and made of plastic. It is lined with newspaper and then filled with a suitable material that is used by the cat for defecation and urination. Commercial cat litter can be purchased, and this consists of small nodules of fuller's earth or clay. Other suitable materials are sand, peat, soil, shredded bark or chippings or cut-up newspaper. The best material to use is that which can be disposed of by being burnt as this is both hygienic and also destroys the eggs of certain internal parasites in the event of these being present.

The kitten needs to be provided with its own place in which to sleep, and there are many different types of bed or basket to choose from in pet shops. For a young kitten, however, a strong cardboard box with fairly high sides but with part of one cut out to make a door is just as suitable. It can be lined first with layers of newspaper and then an old cushion, blankets or other suitable coverings, and these should be washed frequently. Alternatively, a wooden or cardboard box can be laid on its side to make a roofed bed, which has the advantage of screening out any draughts and giving an added feeling of security. The bed should be placed in a warm, safe place near where the members of the household spend most of their time. It has to be said that once the kitten has settled in and grows to adulthood, it will probably suit itself as to where it sleeps. Cats like to seek out the warmest, sunniest and most comfortable spots, irrespective of their official bed or basket.

It is worthwhile right at the start to invest in an elasticated cat collar (which will 'give' if it should become caught in something), with an attached disc engraved with some means of identification. Obviously, if the cat strays from home at some stage, there is a much greater chance of it being returned if it wears a collar carrying an identification disc. Some owners like to attach a little bell to the collar to lessen the cat's success in catching garden birds.

There is likely to be great excitement in a family with children when the day comes to bring home the new kitten. It is essential to resist the temptation just to carry the kitten, even if it is only out to a car. A kitten may look helpless, but if it becomes frightened, as may be the case when it is taken out of its familiar surroundings, it can easily slip out of a person's hands and run away. It would, of course, be dangerous to have a kitten running loose in a moving car. Hence a box of some kind is needed for transport, and a strong cardboard one with high sides is perfectly adequate for a kitten. It needs to be lined with a suitable warm covering (e.g. newspaper and an old towel) and the top should be folded down to make a lid. Some holes should be made in the flaps of the lid for ventilation before leaving home. Alternatively, two boxes can be used, one slightly larger than the other. The larger one needs to have holes made in the base and is inverted over the smaller one to make a lid. The smaller one should be warmly lined, and once the kitten is safely inside the two boxes can be secured together with string. Some people prefer to invest in a manufactured 'cat carrier' basket, which can be purchased from a pet shop. This might seem to be a rather expensive item but will certainly come in useful throughout the lifetime of the cat for visits to the veterinary surgery, etc. A cardboard box is not suitable for the transport of an adult cat as it is not strong enough. Unfortunately, the whole experience of being transported to a new home is likely to be an upsetting one for the kitten. All that can be done is to make sure that the kitten is safe during the journey and to minimize the trauma as far as possible.

Settling In

When the kitten arrives in its new home, it is likely to feel unsettled and anxious at first, and may cry for its mother and brothers and sisters. It should be put in its bed or basket, which is placed in a warm and quiet corner that is free from draughts. A child's soft, furry toy or even a well-covered, warm hot-water bottle will help to reassure the kitten and make it feel more at home. The litter tray needs to be positioned in a suitable secluded place a short distance away from the bed, and it is best to keep the kitten confined to one room at first, which is usually the kitchen. The kitten should be on a floor that is easy to clean and disinfect as, even with a litter tray, there are likely to be 'accidents' at first. Cats are inquisitive and curious animals and the new kitten will be keen to explore its surroundings and find out where everything is. It should be shown its feeding and water bowl and offered a small quantity of familiar appropriate food and drink. The golden rule in feeding is 'little and often', and each time food is consumed, the kitten should be placed on its litter tray. (*See* DIET—Feeding a Kitten as It Grows to Adulthood, page 45, and TRAINING—Toilet Training, page 56.)

The kitten will enjoy receiving plenty of attention and being picked up, petted and played with. Something as simple as a twist of paper tied onto a piece of string and pulled across the floor provides hours of entertainment and other objects will be prodded and investigated. Like all young animals, a kitten needs plenty of rest, and bouts of play and activity are interspersed with frequent sleeping and feeding.

Children in a family will usually be very enthusiastic about the kitten and enjoy playing with, and caring for, their new pet. Kittens are quite vulnerable to injury, however, particularly getting under people's feet and being trodden on, and children must be taught to be careful when handling them. A young child especially must learn to respect the kitten's needs and that it cannot be played with like a soft toy. Kittens have sharp teeth and claws, and may use them if they are being restrained or handled too roughly, and this is obviously unpleasant for both the child and the cat. Young children between the ages of about three and six years should always be supervised when picking up or holding a kitten and should be taught the correct way to do so. The best way to pick up a kitten is to approach it gently and slowly, avoiding any sudden or grabbing movements. After first stroking the kitten, it can be lifted gently with one hand beneath the chest and front legs and the other below the hind end, back legs and tail, so that the weight of the body is fully supported. Neither a kitten nor an adult cat should be lifted around its 'middle' or abdomen (i.e. with both hands placed underneath between the front and hind legs) as this is uncomfortable and unpleasant for the animal. Younger children should also sit down, preferably on the floor, before being allowed to pick up a kitten. This is to avoid the risk of the kitten being dropped from a height, as invariably happens if it uses its claws or teeth because it does not wish to be handled. Of course, it is also important to teach children to wash their hands after handling pets.

If there are babies or toddlers in the family, it may be best to delay having a kitten or cat until they have grown up a little. Children of this age tend to grab and pull at things, and the animal will resent this and react accordingly. It is also difficult to keep a constant eye on things, and it is not unheard of for a horrified parent to find his or her baby playing with the contents of the litter tray or sampling the cat's food. Children are at risk from two diseases (or zoonoses) that can be passed on from cats; these are toxoplasmosis (*see* A-Z OF ILLNESSES, INJURIES AND VETERINARY PROCEDURES, page 220) and visceral larval migrans (*see* PARASITES—Internal Parasites, page 128). The organisms responsible may be present in cat faeces but, with vigilance and scrupulous attention to hygiene, the risks should be slight.

At first a kitten should be kept indoors until it has adjusted to its new surroundings and allowed into the garden only under careful supervision. Someone should accompany the kitten at all times while it is exploring the garden, and the degree of freedom that can be allowed depends upon how safe and secure the area is. A length of string fastened to the collar may provide some reassurance that the kitten will not run away and get lost. Once the kitten is settled and has started to learn to come when its name is called or appear on the doorstep crying to be let in, one may feel more confident about allowing it to come and go when it pleases. There are no hard-and-fast rules about when this time comes, and it is probably best to play safe and supervise the kitten for a longer period of time rather than risk losing a new pet.

Unfortunately, it is not possible to teach a kitten or cat to have any awareness of the dangers presented by road traffic. Many people, especially those living in busy, urban areas, now keep cats permanently indoors to avoid the risk of their pet being run over, injured or killed. Others prefer to take this risk on board and allow the cat to lead a more normal life. One compromise, if suitable space is available in the garden, is to construct an outdoor run and play area for a kitten, enclosed by wire netting. Ideally, there should be height as well as length, with raised platforms and a tree branch on which the kitten can climb and sharpen its claws. There should be a warm, weatherproof box and shade as well as sunshine. This may be a project that would only appeal to a DIY enthusiast but may well be considered worthwhile when it is considered that the lifetime of a cat can be in excess of fifteen years. Of course, it would not be fair to leave a young kitten on its own in a run for long periods of time, but once a cat is older it may be happy to spend a lot of its time in there. Pedigree male stud cats are often kept in similar outdoor accommodation.

If the kitten is coming into a home in which there is already a resident cat or dog (or both), then precautions are needed in introducing the newcomer. An older cat is likely to resent the newcomer at first and to express its anger by growling or merely ignoring the kitten. The situation can be eased by lavishing attention on the resident cat and taking very little notice of the newcomer while it is present. This is to reassure the adult cat that its place has not been usurped in its owners' affections. Occasionally, there may be more extreme reactions from the older cat, such as a breakdown in toilet training. Usually, the resident cat ignores the new kitten and initially rebuffs its friendly overtures with growling or a cuff if it gets too close. Generally, this situation does not persist, and the older cat becomes more tolerant and eventually puts up with a certain amount of playful behaviour from the youngster. The new kitten will certainly wish to be accepted by the older cat and will normally be prepared to accept a subordinate position. Rarely, the situation does not improve and aggression continues. If this is the case, it is best to try to find another home for the kitten rather than prolong the conflict.

It is to be hoped that owners of a dog will have assessed its character and will feel confident of success if they decide to introduce a kitten or cat. Most dogs have a tendency to chase any animal that runs away, including cats. This tendency to chase cats should have been checked during the dog's training period. It is obviously essential to take great care when introducing the dog to the kitten, i.e. holding it by the collar and not leaving the two animals alone together while the reaction can be assessed. A dog may often be jealous at first, so, again, it is necessary to give it plenty of affection, attention and reassurance. Generally, after a time, the dog accepts the new arrival quite happily and often the two become good friends. More often than not, it is the cat that eventually becomes the undisputed ruler of the household. Conflicts that might arise at meal times should be avoided by feeding the pair separately and firmly discouraging each from raiding the other's bowl.

Small animals that can be regarded as the natural prey of a cat, particularly cage birds, mice or hamsters and fish, are not likely to be at risk from a young kitten but certainly will be when they grow up. It is not safe to allow a cat any access to smaller animals (including rabbits and guinea pigs) that may, in any event, feel frightened by its presence. A cat can be quite persistent and cunning in its determination to get at smaller pets. Anyone who has observed a cat sitting intently in front of a budgie's cage or a fish tank, watching the occupant's every move, can be left in no doubt as to what its intentions are.

Taking Home an Adult Cat

Many of the factors that apply to bringing home a kitten are relevant to an adult cat (*see* page 21). Similar preparations need to be made with regard to providing a bed, a supply of food and a litter tray, etc. It is necessary, however, to borrow or purchase a proper cat-carrying basket as a cardboard box is not sufficiently strong or secure.

The way in which the settling-in process proceeds very much depends upon the nature of each individual cat. An adult cat has obviously gained experiences of life that may have been mainly good or mainly bad. It may be trusting and affectionate towards people or shy and wary, and all this will influence how it behaves in its new home. If the cat is not used to using a litter tray it may be reluctant to learn, and it may resent being fitted with a collar. It is certainly advisable to keep the cat indoors for the first few days until it has adjusted to its new surroundings, but the length of time needed is difficult to gauge. Obviously, a problem arises if the cat is accustomed to going out of doors to relieve itself, and it is much more difficult to control the movements of an adult animal than a kitten. It is a good idea therefore to introduce the cat to the garden and the immediate surroundings of the house on a lead or longer line attached to its collar. The cat should be given plenty of time to investigate and explore its environment and to become familiar with the route back home. When the cat is let out for the first time on its own, it is best to do this when you know that it is hungry, i.e. just before it expects a meal. The cat should have had time to appreciate receiving regular, appetizing meals, and it is to be hoped that it will be strongly motivated to return rather than to explore and possibly become lost.

All being well, the cat will appreciate its good fortune in finding a new home and people to look after it, and the settling-in process will proceed smoothly. The golden rule is probably to persevere with patience and kindness but, at the same time, to let the cat know what you expect of it in terms of acceptable behaviour. It is a good idea for the cat to have a health check carried out by a veterinary surgeon so that any problems can be identified and treated. At the same time, advice on a suitable programme of worming can be obtained and arrangements made for vaccination and neutering, if these are needed.

DIET

Vitamins and Minerals

The cat is a true carnivore and in the wild catches and kills small rodents and birds and consumes the whole of its prey to fulfil its nutritional requirements. The prey animal consists mainly of protein with a smaller amount of fat and a considerable proportion (90 per cent) of fluid. By eating the whole of the animal, including the contents of the gut and the bones, the cat obtains sufficient quantities of vitamins and minerals such as calcium. The most important nutritional requirements are therefore for protein and fat, and cats require proportionately greater amounts than is the case for dogs. Also, unlike dogs, cats are not able to utilize carbohydrates as an energy source to any significant extent. In fact, carbohydrates, contained in such foods as cereals, bread and potatoes, are not needed at all in the diet of the cat but can be given in small amounts in a form that has been cooked. The reason for this is that cats are unable to digest starch unless it is in cooked food. The best food to offer is one with a high protein content, which is essential for growth and repair of tissues and is also used to provide energy. There should also be some fat present as this is a more readily converted source of energy than protein. The main vitamins required by cats are A, D and B. They are able to manufacture vitamin C within the body and apparently do not need vitamin K. Cats are not able to change the precursors of vitamin A (called carotenoids and found in vegetables such as carrots as well as other plants) into the vitamin. They must therefore obtain vitamin A directly from food, and good sources are liver, oily fish and cod liver oil. However, since vitamin A is fat-soluble, i.e. it can be stored and concentrated in the body, it is needed only sparingly and in small quantities. Indeed, it is important to avoid giving an excess of all the fat-soluble vitamins, A, D and E, as this can lead to disorders and deformities of the skeleton and organs (hypervitaminosis). In general, an adult cat is unlikely to be deficient in any vitamins if it is being fed a balanced and varied diet, and there is no need to add manufactured supplements.

The most important minerals needed are calcium and phosphorus, which are usually present in sufficient quantities in a good diet. An excess of minerals can cause painful disorders of the skeleton and joints, particularly in growing kittens, hence supplements should not normally be given.

There are circumstances when supplements of minerals and vitamins may be prescribed for a cat by a veterinary surgeon. Cats that have been ill and are reluctant to eat, or those that are debilitated for some reason, growing kittens and pregnant females may occasionally require such supplements in their diet. It is essential that this need is determined by a veterinary surgeon. The cat's owner should not give vitamin or mineral supplements without obtaining expert advice.

Many people in Great Britain now eat a vegetarian diet. Those who are dog and cat owners sometimes ask if such a diet is a suitable one for their pet. The answer to this is that while a dog can be satisfactorily nourished on a vegetarian diet because it is more omnivorous, a cat is a true carnivore and needs protein and fat derived from animal sources or else it will become ill. These differences do not relate to the food that the animals can be persuaded to eat but to internal metabolic processes within cells and tissues.

It has already been stated that cats must obtain vitamin A from animal sources. In contrast to dogs, they are not able to convert the precursors of the vitamin, called carotenoids, into vitamin A. Both dogs and cats have a dietary need for ten essential amino acids (the units of which proteins are composed), and these can be found in both animal and plant foods. There is, however, another vital amino acid, called taurine, that many mammals, including dogs, are able to produce within the body from the other amino acids consumed in food. The cat does not have this ability and must obtain taurine from animal protein where it is present in higher quantities. (A deficiency in this amino acid leads to degeneration of the light-receiving layer of the eye called the retina and subsequent blindness.) Fats from both plant and animal sources are a source of energy and contain essential fatty acids that are necessary for many internal biochemical reactions vital for life. Of particular importance in the diet of both dogs and cats is linoleic acid, which is one of three essential fatty acids. Linoleic acid is found in animal fats and vegetable oils such as corn oil. However, dogs are able to manufacture the other two essential fatty acids, which are arachidonic and linolenic acid, within the body. Dietary linoleic acid is converted into the other two essential fatty acids when needed, and dogs can obtain this from either plant or animal sources. Cats, on the other hand, are unable to convert linoleic acid and must obtain linolenic acid and arachidonic acid in their food. These are only found in the tissues of animals. It can be seen, therefore, that while cats may enjoy eating other types of food, they lack the necessary internal adaptations to be anything other than carnivores and become ill if they are given an unsuitable diet.

Raw or Cooked Food

Obviously, in the wild it is natural for cats to consume raw food and the whole of the prey animal is eaten. Studies have shown that cats may have slightly better rates of growth and reproductive success if fed on a suitable varied raw diet. The difference is, however, extremely small, and there are good reasons why certain foods should not be given raw. For instance, raw egg white contains two substances, one of which reduces the availability of a particular B vitamin (biotin) while the other inhibits the digestion of protein in the stomach. Eggs, therefore, which are an excellent food for cats, should always be cooked as this destroys the unhelpful substances. Meat can be given raw but, unfortunately, this is one of the ways in which the parasitic organism *Toxoplasma gondii*, the cause of toxoplasmosis (*see* A-Z OF ILLNESSES, INJURIES AND VETERINARY PROCEDURES, page 220) in people, is passed on. Cooking destroys this organism and also some other harmful bacteria that might be present and enhances the flavour of the food. Meat or fish for a cat should be cooked for the shortest time possible, e.g. lightly boiled, in order to preserve essential vitamins.

Commercially prepared and tinned cat food is sterilized in order to destroy potentially harmful microorganisms. Manufacturers generally add vitamins (especially vitamin B) in carefully controlled amounts to ensure that the cat receives the quantity needed.

In the wild, a cat starts to eat its prey soon after having made a kill, while the body is still warm. Studies have shown that cats prefer their food to be slightly warm (about 40°C or blood heat) but usually will not touch it if it is too hot. Of course, most cats happily accept food served straight from the can at room temperature. However, if a cat needs to be tempted to eat, e.g. during or after illness, warming a small quantity of its favourite food is often helpful.

Bones

In the wild, cats eat the bones of their prey, and this is extremely important as these provide essential calcium. Domestic cats can obtain calcium in a different form, so do not need to eat bones, although many enjoy doing so. Since cats are careful eaters and are much more inclined to chew their food, they do not usually suffer from problems when they eat bones. They are, for instance, far less likely to swallow sharp fragments of bone than dogs, which are inclined to rush and gulp down their food. Occasionally, a chop or other bone may become impaled on the cat's sharp teeth or wedged in its mouth in some way. Irregular or brittle bones that may splinter are best avoided and the best type to give a cat are raw limb bones. Chewing is good for the cat, helping to keep its teeth in good order and preventing dental problems. However, chewing the dried type of cat food or one of the many types of manufactured 'chew' are just as effective in this respect as giving a bone. Sharp fish bones may cause problems for a cat and are best removed from its food.

Water

A cat should have unrestricted access to clean, fresh drinking water at all times unless the animal is vomiting (*see* A-Z OF ILL-

NESSES, INJURIES AND VETERINARY PROCEDURES, page 223). Cats need to drink in order to replenish water that has been eliminated from the body through normal functions such as urination. In the wild state, cats obtain a high proportion of the moisture they need from their prey and may drink relatively little water. Similarly, domestic cats that eat meals with a high moisture content, such as tinned food or home-prepared meat in gravy, may also have a low intake of water. However, cats are not always adept at adjusting the amount of water they need to drink according to the moisture content of their food. Some cats that are fed on commercial, dried foods do not receive enough moisture in their diet but do not compensate for this by drinking more water. Unfortunately, this can contribute towards the development of a blockage of the urinary tract in male cats and a severe disorder called feline urological syndrome (FUS) (*see* A-Z OF ILLNESSES, INJURIES AND VETERINARY PROCEDURES, page 185).

Many cats seem to prefer drinking milk and, of course, this is composed largely of water and is also a good source of protein, fat and calcium. However, milk is more correctly a food rather than a drink and should not be given as a substitute for water. There is no harm in giving a cat a daily ration of milk if it enjoys it and it does not upset its digestion. There is a widespread belief that milk or even cream is the correct drink to give a cat. It may come as a surprise to learn that quite a number of adult cats, particularly Siamese and some other Eastern breeds, have a digestive intolerance to cow's milk. It appears that they may be allergic to a particular protein present in the milk and suffer digestive upset and diarrhoea (*see* A-Z OF ILLNESSES, INJURIES AND VETERINARY PROCEDURES, page 173). Other cats may be deficient in the enzyme lactase, which is needed to break down the sugar (lactose) present in the milk. It may be necessary to withhold other dairy products, particularly cheese, from a cat that suffers from this disorder.

Home-prepared Foods

In contrast to dogs, cats enjoy a varied diet, and giving them different sorts of food is the best way to ensure that they stay healthy and obtain all the vitamins and minerals that they need. All kinds of meat can be given, either braised in gravy or lightly boiled, perhaps with a small quantity of mashed potato added. The meat does not need to be too lean since cats have a need for fat in their diet. Liver is very popular with cats and is a good source of vitamin A. Some cats show a great preference for liver, but it is not good for them to have it too frequently as this might result in an excess buildup of vitamin A, which can be the cause of skeletal deformities. Chicken, game of all kinds and rabbit are all enjoyed by cats, and some of the bones can be given as well to provide calcium. Kidney, heart, tripe and lungs are suitable foods to give occasionally, although lungs do not have a high protein content. Cooked but not raw fish should be given on a regular basis, and it is a good source of various minerals including iodine. Oily fish is a rich source of vitamins A, D and E and can be offered to cats occasionally. Dairy products, particularly milk and cheese, are very popular with most cats and are an excellent source of calcium, protein and fat. A balanced diet consists of small quantities of all these types of food, a different one being offered each day.

Meals based solely on meat are not suitable since, while supplying plenty of protein and fat, they are deficient in calcium, vitamin A and phosphorus. To restore the balance, a small quantity of sterilized, powdered bone meal (which contains phosphorus and calcium), cod liver oil (vitamins A, D and E) and yeast (vitamin B) can be added to the food. It is best to seek veterinary advice if there is cause for concern about the diet of a cat before adding any extra vitamin and mineral supplements to its food. It should always be borne in mind that if a cat is allowed to roam freely it may well be obtaining food elsewhere or even hunting and eating prey animals.

Cats are capable of developing quite exotic and expensive tastes if given any encouragement. There is no harm in occasionally offering tinned fish such as tuna or sardines or a few prawns if the owner's budget is sufficiently accommodating. Manufacturers also make luxury 'gourmet' foods that are very tasty and highly acceptable to cats. These are generally intended to be offered as an occasional treat for cats that are eating a balanced and varied diet.

Commercially Prepared Cat Foods

A view is sometimes expressed among pet owners that the food given to dogs and cats should always be home-prepared and that manufactured products are a poor substitute. In the same way, some people eschew all manufactured 'convenience' foods for themselves and perhaps feel that as their pet is a part of the family its meals should be prepared in the same way. In fact, as has already been noted, cats have quite specific nutritional needs and a great deal of scientific research has been carried out to establish exactly what these are. In this way, reputable manufacturers of cat food ensure that their product is prepared to a high standard and contains the correct balance of protein, fat, vitamins and minerals. So great is the popularity of cats as pets, and so fierce the level of competition in the food market, that no reputable manufacturer can afford to compromise the standard of its product. In fact, it is probably more correct to say that since many people do give their pets manufactured foods cats are now much better fed than they were in the past. When little was known about the dietary requirements of cats, they were often fed on scraps or leftovers, frequently with an over-reliance on white fish. In this way, some cats were inadequately nourished and suffered from deficiency disorders and, consequently, a lowered life expectancy.

Manufactured cat food is now available in three forms. Wet or moist food is the familiar sort available in tins and has a high water content, in the order of 80 per cent. Semi-moist food is usually available in sealed, strong plastic bags, and the water content is in the order of 30 per cent. Dry food is usually sold in cardboard cartons, and the water content is much lower and does not exceed 10 per cent.

These foods are normally enjoyed by most cats, and some owners like to offer a combination of all three. If the moist food is offered exclusively, it is necessary to give the cat something suitable on which to chew to ensure that its teeth remain in good order. Both the semi-moist and the dried food contain insufficient amounts of water.

It is especially important to ensure that the cat has access to fresh drinking water at all times if this type of food is usually given. The dried and semi-moist meals are very suitable for those who wish to allow their cat continual access to food so that it can help itself whenever it pleases. Studies have shown that most cats like to eat 'a little and often' and the majority take only the quantity that they need. The drier types of food do not deteriorate quickly or become stale and so are ideal for feeding in this way. Moist types of food, whether tinned or home-prepared, should not be left out for any length of time, and anything left needs to be thrown away fairly promptly. In the warm environment of modern centrally heated homes harmful bacteria and their toxins can soon proliferate on this type of food, which also attracts bluebottles and houseflies. Usually, an owner gets to know the habits of a pet cat and can estimate the amount of food needed quite accurately. If the contents of a tin or other food are not all used at once, they can be safely stored in a refrigerator.

Some experts advise against feeding too much of the dried type of food because of its possible contribution to feline urological syndrome (*see* A-Z OF ILLNESSES, INJURIES AND VETERINARY PROCEDURES, page 185). There is not a fault with the food itself; the problem lies in the failure of some cats to increase their intake of water when eating this kind of meal. If water intake is inadequate, the urine becomes more concentrated and there may be precipitation of crystalline material, which forms an obstruction in the urethra. The disorder affects male cats, which have a relatively narrow urethra. It is thought that dried cat food is only a contributory factor in the development of this disorder. The main cause is believed to be infection with a virus, but a cat that has had feline urological syndrome in the past may require a special diet and generally should not be fed on dried foods. However, many cats thrive on and enjoy dried food, which also provides excellent chewing exercise to ensure the health of the teeth and gums.

Eating Grass

Like dogs, many cats occasionally eat grass, and it is believed that in the wild they may do this to obtain vitamins and minerals, such as folic acid, which may be lacking in the diet. (In the wild state, cats also eat the gut contents of their prey, which usually consists of partly digested plant material.) A cat is sometimes sick after it has eaten grass, and so the purpose may be to provoke vomiting in certain circumstances. The animal may be feeling uncomfortable because of the presence of a fur ball in the stomach (*see* A-Z OF ILLNESSES, INJURIES AND VETERINARY PROCEDURES, page 191) or because it has eaten something that has upset its digestion. In a similar way, grass may act as roughage or as a natural laxative, helping to prevent the discomfort of constipation (*see* A-Z OF ILLNESSES, page 166).

Eating grass is a common habit among cats, and some may even sample house plants and need to be trained not to do so. A cat that is kept permanently in the house will appreciate being supplied with a turf of fresh grass. Alternatively, a tray can be seeded with grass and grown indoors especially for the cat. Providing alternatives will probably make it easier to prevent house plants from being nibbled or knocked over.

Feeding a Kitten as It Grows to Adulthood

As noted previously, a kitten should be about eight weeks old (or even a little younger) before it arrives in its new home. At this age, it should be used to feeding and lapping milk and no longer be dependent upon its mother for nourishment. The golden rule in feeding a kitten is to offer a 'little and often'. Between the ages of seven to twelve weeks, three to four teaspoonfuls of good quality, high protein food should be given as four meals each day along with small drinks of milk. It is best to offer the food that the kitten is used to at the start and to introduce changes very gradually. If the kitten develops diarrhoea, the new food should be stopped and if the condition persists veterinary attention is needed.

Manufacturers produce tasty foods for kittens, and these are easy to give as they contain exactly the right nutritional elements. If a kitten is being fed exclusively on home-produced foods, it may be necessary to add one or two drops of cod liver oil and a small quantity ($1/4$ teaspoonful) of yeast and sterilized bone meal to one of its daily meals to ensure that it receives the necessary vitamins and minerals. Alternatively, proprietary vitamin and mineral supplements can be obtained from a veterinary clinic, but it is essential to seek expert advice before one of these is used. At first, the milk offered to a kitten can be a proprietary make formulated for cats, with a gradual change to ordinary cows' milk as the animal becomes older.

Between the ages of three to six months, the amount of food offered at each feed can be increased slightly, and the number of daily meals reduced to three. After this age, slightly more food can be given and the number of meals reduced to two. The young cat is now well on its way to adulthood, and, while there are no hard-and-fast rules about this, many owners like to give their cat one small feed in the morning and a larger main meal in the evening. In fact, surveys have shown that the majority of cats, given unlimited access to food, eat small quantities every two to three hours. If food is left out for a cat, it may well choose to eat in this way, regardless of the decisions of its owner.

As with all young animals, kittens require a proportionately greater amount of food relative to their body weight than adult cats as they are growing so rapidly. As a guide, a young, weaned kitten aged six weeks needs about $3^{1}/_{2}$ ounces of food each day, increasing to 7 ounces at ten weeks. Adult cats generally need between 7-9 ounces of food every day but individual requirements vary considerably, depending upon their level of activity, age and living conditions. Also, at particular times an individual cat may require more or less food. Examples include a mother cat nursing new kittens, which needs about three times as much food because of the tremendous demands being made upon her. In contrast, a cat forced into inactivity, perhaps as a result of a limb injury, needs slightly less food until it is able to resume its normal lifestyle. An aged cat that spends most of its time sleeping in the sun needs less food than it did when it was young and active. Neutered cats need less food than intact ones and have an increased tendency to become obese.

Overfeeding and Obesity

A recent study showed that at least half the pet dogs and cats in the British Isles are overweight and obesity is a common problem. As with people, cats do not become obese overnight; the increase in weight usually takes place gradually and may hardly be noticed at first. If the ribs cannot be felt, the cat is overweight, and if the size of its body makes its head and legs seem too small it is obese. Any animal that takes in more food each day than is needed to satisfy its energy requirements is likely to lay down fat reserves and eventually become obese. At one time, cats were very good at regulating their food intake and did not eat to excess. Several possible explanations for the present increase in obesity have been offered and in each individual case there may be a combination of factors involved.

Firstly, manufactured foods prepared for cats are a great deal more tasty and attractive than they were in the past, and there are now 'gourmet' meals available. Cats are more likely to gorge themselves on this type of food simply because they like the taste. Secondly, it has become increasingly more common to keep cats indoors all the time because of the dangers presented by crowded, busy roads. Such cats are likely to be less active and, in some cases, even bored, and may be inclined to

48

eat more than they need as a result. Thirdly, owners are very inclined to overestimate the needs of their pet and to assume that because the cat is avidly eating all of a tasty type of food, and perhaps asking for more, that this must be what it requires. Finally, many people derive pleasure from giving a pet a tasty titbit of food, often a portion of the family meal, and spoiling it in this way. This is a mistaken act of kindness if the pet then becomes obese. Very fat cats are likely to be lethargic and may find difficulty and discomfort in moving around. Arthritic problems are also likely to be made worse if a cat is over-weight.

Overweight cats are usually well cared for and much loved and are likely to be the ones regularly seen at a veterinary clinic (for vaccination boosters, etc). It is therefore often the veterinary surgeon who first alerts the owners to the fact that their cat is overweight and is the one who suggests a slimming routine. Usually the cat is weighed to discover the extent of the problem, and a correct target weight will be established. There is likely to be some discussion about the current eating habits of the cat, and total honesty is needed here on the part of the owners. When the daily amount of food being given is examined critically, many people are astonished to realise how much they are overfeeding their pet. In some cases, cutting out all the extras and titbits along with a small reduction in the normal meal may be all that is needed to bring about the desired weight loss. In other instances, it may be suggested that the cat should be put on a specially formulated 'light' diet that is lower in fat. The aim is to achieve a gradual weight loss by a sensible reduction in the amount of food given rather than to starve the cat.

It may be suggested that the cat is weighed once a week. This can be done at home by the owner weighing himself (or herself) first and then repeating the process while holding the cat. The difference between the two is the weight of the cat and, while it cannot be totally accurate, it is to be hoped it will give some idea of how things are progressing. After a period of weeks, the weight loss should be able to be seen and felt, even in a very furry cat. The veterinary surgeon may wish to see the cat again for a more accurate weighing. Once the target weight has been achieved, the food allowance may be gradually increased to a maintenance level. Weekly weighing at home can then ensure that the problem does not recur.

Underfeeding, Weight Loss, Feeding a Sick Cat

In normal circumstances it is unlikely that a pet cat will be underfed. A healthy hungry kitten or cat will eat its food with enthusiasm and ask for more if it has not had enough. Routine weighing can detect weight loss, and this will eventually be noticed when petting the cat. Unexplained weight loss is a cause for concern, and the cat should be taken to a veterinary surgeon so that the cause can be investigated. It may be accompanied by other symptoms indicative of an underlying illness.

Stray cats and kittens that have been living rough are frequently severely malnourished. In the case of a kitten, this can have serious consequences for its growth and development, particularly if it has consistently failed to receive sufficient food. Even if the kitten is subsequently fed correctly, after a certain age it may have lost too much ground and its growth can remain stunted. Adult cats that are seriously undernourished usually look painfully thin and in poor condition. The fur may appear dull and matted, and the ribs and backbone are prominent and easily felt beneath the skin, which lacks subcutaneous fat. A cat in this state may have a heavy burden of intestinal worm parasites (*see* PARASITES—Internal Parasites, page 128) which weaken it further as it has no reserves or resistance to them. It is likely to be harbouring skin parasites, particularly fleas and ear mites (*see* PARASITES—External Parasites, pages 136, 140), which can be a further cause of serious debility. The cat is particularly vulnerable to bacterial and viral infections while in such a weakened state and is more likely to succumb to any form of illness. If its condition is very severe, it may be apathetic and have insufficient energy to resist the ministrations of people that it might otherwise not welcome.

A cat that is obviously in a severely weakened and undernourished state requires veterinary attention and may need to be put on a special feeding routine. One of the animal welfare charities, such as the RSPCA or SSPCA, will take care of the cat in case of any difficulty. In less severe cases, where the cat is willing and able to take food, there is no harm in giving it a good meal before deciding on appropriate further action.

It is sometimes necessary to employ considerable ingenuity and patience to persuade an ill or convalescent cat to eat. If a cat is refusing to eat, the best food to try in the first instance is a small amount of one that is a known favourite. At this stage, the aim is to get the cat to accept some food and not to worry too much about whether it is balanced or not. Foods with a strong taste are likely to prove more successful, e.g. fish such as sardines, pilchards or tuna or meat or liver in a flavoured gravy. This is particularly important if the cat is suffering from any respiratory disorder or nasal congestion, when its senses of smell and taste are impaired. Food should be warmed gently and milk offered if it is normally enjoyed by the cat. Smearing a little of the food on to the tongue or on to the nose, from where it will be licked off, may persuade the cat to sample the food. Specially formulated and highly nutritious foods designed for sick cats can be obtained from veterinary clinics and may be worth trying if the usual diet is rejected.

If all else fails, it may be necessary to attempt gently to force-feed a sick cat. This can be attempted only if the animal is weak but conscious and it is time-consuming, requiring care and patience. Liquid foods such as milk or a meat soup can be given by means of a disposable plastic syringe or eye dropper. If possible, two people should be involved and one should gently hold the cat from behind with the hands around its front legs. It may be easier to wrap the cat in a towel, just leaving its head free. The person doing the feeding should take hold of the cat by the scruff of the neck and tilt its head backwards so that the nose points upwards. The syringe is then inserted gently at the side of the mouth and one or two drops of food allowed to trickle out. Only a little should be given at each mouthful, with time allowed for the cat to swallow and take a breath. If the cat coughs or makes a choking sound, its head must be lowered immediately. Stiffer food of a paste-like consistency can be given in this way or using the handle of a teaspoon to insert a small quantity into the side of the mouth. The main danger with this form of feeding is the risk of inhalation of food and consequent development of pneumonia (*see* A-Z OF ILLNESSES, page 207), which is often fatal. It is essential that only small amounts of food are given and to recognize at the outset that the process is likely to take some time. In fact, a cat will usually swallow only a small amount of food given in this way, and in order to try and make sure it receives enough, the whole operation needs to be repeated every two or three hours. It is worth persevering, however, as it is to be hoped the cat will soon feel well enough to start eating in the normal way.

Training

Training a Kitten

For many people, one of the great attractions of cats is their independent nature. However, it must be appreciated that this means that it is less easy to train a cat compared to a dog. A dog usually wishes to please its owners and to earn their praise, whereas a cat's main concern is itself. Fortunately, a cat needs less training than a dog and is usually far more unobtrusive. All that is usually needed is some firm and consistent handling from the start and it is largely a matter of good common sense. In some cases, an owner may need to be firm for quite a time as a cat may try to assert itself and fail to realize who is supposed to be in charge.

Cats soon learn to respond to the inflections of their owner's voice and a cross tone can be an effective deterrent, although it is a mistake to shout as this may simply frighten a kitten. Also, they intensely dislike loud sharp noises, so clapping the hands or striking the top of a table with a rolled-up newspaper are highly effective. Simple command words like 'no', 'get down', 'bad', 'out', etc, should be used as a part of training. Then it is a matter of consistently checking bad and undesirable behaviour as soon as, and each time, it appears, so that the kitten gradually learns what is acceptable. For instance, if it uses its claws or teeth when being played with, the owner should say 'No' sharply and perhaps tap the kitten's nose or paw with a finger. The kitten must be told to 'Get down' each time it climbs on a chair, if this is not acceptable to its owners, and lifted down onto the floor. One of the most annoying and destructive habits that cats can have is to sharpen their claws on furniture. Claw-sharpening is part of the repertoire of normal behaviour, its purpose in the wild being to ensure that the claws are in good order for climbing and for fighting, if the occasion arises. It is the front ones that are sharpened, and the cat does this by standing or sitting on its hind legs and raking its extended claws down a suitable surface. Claw-sharpening also helps to mark the cat's territory and apparently helps to impress and repel possible rivals.

To correct this behaviour when it is applied to the furniture, it is necessary to be very firm and possibly even tap the kitten with a rolled-up newspaper. Alternatively, the kitten should be sternly told off, or a sudden noise made at the moment it starts to behave in this way. The kitten should be provided with a scratching post on which it is allowed to use its claws. This can be purchased from a pet shop or one can be made at home. It consists of a firmly anchored upright post, usually set in a wide, square or rectangular base, and covered with some suitable material, such as carpet, rope, sacking or canvas. Alternatively, a log, branch or fence post nailed to a suitable base can be provided if the cat's owners do not object to having this in the house. Each time the kitten makes any attempt to claw the furniture, it should be firmly rebuked and then removed to the post and its front paws placed on this so that it can learn to use this instead. It is also a good idea to play games with the kitten, getting it to chase a piece of paper tied to a string up and around the scratching post. In this way it will dig its claws into the post and be encouraged to use that rather than the furniture for this natural aspect of feline behaviour.

Toilet Training

In general, cats are clean and fastidious animals, and their normal behaviour is to pass urine and faeces in loose soil that is first dug and scratched out to make a hollow. Once the cat has finished, it uses its paws to cover its traces and scratches with more soil over the toilet area. In the first three weeks of life, kittens are relatively helpless and more or less confined to their bed or box. The mother cat licks them frequently and swallows the waste materials that her offspring pass. In fact, the kittens are stimulated to eliminate urine and faeces by their mother's licking of the genital and anal openings. At the age of about three weeks, the kittens are moving around more and starting to explore the area outside the bed. This coincides with the time when the mother ceases to clean up the motions that the kittens pass and she may lift them onto the litter tray herself. In any event, the kittens are 'programmed' to use a suitable substrate in which to relieve themselves and will often choose to use a litter tray quite naturally.

The most successful way to proceed is to keep the kitten in one room (usually the kitchen) until it has learnt to use the litter tray. The tray should be placed in a quiet, secluded corner at a suitable distance from the bed. It may be a good idea to place the tray on a few sheets of newspaper or in a *shallow* cardboard box as the kitten may scratch and scatter the contents. The kitten should be placed on the litter tray at frequent intervals, particularly on awakening from a sleep and immediately following a meal. (When the kitten begins to eat and food descends into its stomach, there is an automatic passage of digested material along the bowel caused by the operation of the 'gastrocolic reflex'.) Most young mammals have little control over their bladder and bowels at first but rapidly acquire this as they develop. Accidents are inevitable with very young kittens, but many will be well on the way to becoming trained by the time they are taken to a new home. The move to a new home is, of course, unsettling for a new kitten, and owners should be patient over the mistakes that occur. If the kitten is seen to be urinating or defecating in the wrong place, it should be told off sharply and immediately taken to the litter tray. The mess must be cleaned up thoroughly and disinfected—if any odour remains, the kitten may use the same spot again. The litter must be changed frequently, and certainly before it becomes soiled and smelly as cats are fastidious and may refuse to use a tray in these circumstances. Ideally, soiled cat litter should always be burnt and it may help to choose a type that is readily combustible. It should not be placed on the compost heap because the eggs of some internal parasites (*see* PARASITES—Internal Parasites, page 128) may be present which are very resistant to decay and could potentially be ingested by people, particularly children. Rubber gloves should be worn when changing the litter and the tray should be washed and disinfected.

Occasionally, a kitten or cat is reluctant to use a tray because it dislikes the smell of a litter that has been treated with a chemical deodorizer. It is worthwhile changing the type of litter used to see if this encourages the kitten to use the tray. In addition, proprietary preparations are available that can be sprinkled on to the litter and that attract the kitten to use the tray. If the eventual aim is for the kitten to relieve itself out of doors, it may help to sprinkle some garden soil onto the litter from the start. Soil can itself be used as litter although there may be a problem with disposal.

Some cats quite naturally make the transition from using a litter tray to performing out of doors. Others are reluctant to use anything except a tray once they have been trained to do so. If this is the case, it may help to move the litter tray gradually towards the door, just a few inches each day, until it is eventually placed outside. This is best accomplished in warm, dry weather when the door can be left open. Once the kitten is using the tray outside, a little used litter can be tipped onto an appropriate place in the garden. It should be appreciated that there is nothing more annoying for someone who is a keen gardener than to have a cat digging in the soil and disturbing plants or bulbs. While the owners may not mind too much about their own garden, neighbours may object and there is no guarantee that a cat will stay on its own patch. So, depending upon individual circumstances, it may be advisable to encourage a kitten just to use the litter tray. In any event, it is best to provide a tray for use at night and in bad weather as cats are great lovers of comfort and may prefer not to go out when it is cold and wet.

Learning Its Name

A cat is not so likely to respond and come when its name is called as a dog, unless this suits its purpose at the time. The name chosen for a kitten when it arrives at its new home should be spoken frequently from the start, especially while the owners are playing with it and encouraging it to come to them. The kitten can be rewarded by being praised and petted and given a tasty titbit of food if it comes when its name is called during play. The same approach can subsequently be used once the kitten is allowed outside. The owner should stand at the door and call to the kitten to come in from the garden, rewarding it when it does so. The best that can be hoped for is to encourage the kitten to come in this way, and the system works well if the animal is not overfed and enjoys the reward that is offered. By the time the kitten has grown to adulthood, it will probably have started to evolve a routine of its own. It will certainly know its meal times and will appear regularly for these, and will often show quite predictable behaviour so that its owners have a good idea where it is at any particular time.

Walking on a Lead

A cat can learn to walk on a lead if training is started while it is still a kitten. Some breeds are particularly successful to train in this respect, notably Siamese cats. It is safer to use a harness and lead rather than a collar, and a suitable one can be purchased from a pet shop along with a cat lead. At first the kitten should be allowed to get used to the feeling of wearing the harness (which must have adjustable straps to allow for growth) in the house. The lead may then be clipped on and the kitten allowed to pull it around and play with it while being closely supervised. The next stage is for a person to pick up the end of the lead but follow the kitten wherever it wants to go rather than attempt to direct movement. Once the kitten has got used to this, an attempt can be made to persuade it to walk with the person holding the lead. It should be coaxed to walk by the person's side—never dragged or pulled along but praised and rewarded with a titbit when it gets things right. The kitten can be taught not to run ahead by giving a sharp tug on the lead, accompanied by a firm 'No'; it should eventually learn to remain beside the person.

Once these skills have been mastered inside the house, they can be put into practice in the garden. Initially the kitten may need plenty of reassurance once in the garden. It should be picked up and carried if it appears frightened and only put down for a moment or two at first. Walks can become more ambitious as the kitten matures and gains confidence. If a cat can be taught to walk on a lead it can be exercised outside, even if normally kept indoors because of the dangers presented by road traffic.

Using a Cat Flap or Cat Door

A cat door or flap is a very useful device that allows a cat freedom to come and go more or less as it pleases. It consists of a small opening, about 15 centimetres square, set low down in an external door of the house, usually a back one that opens into the garden. The opening is guarded by some sort of hinged flap, which is pushed by the cat using its head and drops back into position once the animal has passed through. The manner in which the flap is opened varies, depending upon the type of cat door. The simplest type is hinged at the top and can be pushed from both sides. Another kind can be pushed open only from the inside and to re-enter the cat has to learn how to raise the flap with a paw. An even more sophisticated type is usually locked but the flap is released by a magnetized device attached to the cat's collar.

Some cats readily learn to use a cat flap while others need a little more persuasion. The best age to introduce the kitten to this is when it has gained in confidence and is sure of its surroundings, i.e. at about three months old.

At first the flap can be fixed open permanently and a game played in which the cat is persuaded to chase a toy through the hole. Or it can be coaxed through by its owner holding a favourite titbit on the other side of the opening. Once the cat is passing in and out quite happily, the flap can be gradually lowered until it has to push to create a large enough space through which to pass. As long as it is not frightened and no force is used, the cat can be shown how to push the flap with its head.

There were design problems with some of the earlier types of cat flap, which were inclined to rattle and to let in draughts and rain in windy, wet weather. Many of these problems have now been removed, although it is advantageous if a cat flap can be fitted on a door in a fairly sheltered position. One other disadvantage is that stray or neighbouring cats have been known to use cat doors and to enter a house uninvited. The most sophisticated type, which is activated by a device on the resident cat's collar, usually solves this problem.

Training an Adult Cat

An adult cat comes to its new home with a set of established and ingrained behaviour patterns. If the cat has previously been in a good home, it will be well behaved and settle in happily into the household routine. If it has not been so fortunate, however, it may have some bad habits, such as not being toilet-trained, scratching at furniture, jumping on worktops, etc. Training should be much the same as for a kitten, using a mild form of 'shock treatment' or aversion therapy when undesirable behaviour is witnessed. These tactics include making a sudden loud noise or even squirting the cat with cold water from a water pistol, which is particularly effective if the animal does not see where this is coming from. Although this may sound unkind, usually only one or two 'shocks' are necessary for the behaviour to cease. Naturally, there is a fine balance to be struck between frightening a new pet and merely deterring it from behaving antisocially. It is important to give the cat plenty of reassurance and attention and to make sure that it has its own places and spaces in the home where it is allowed to go and to praise it when it behaves correctly.

Sometimes, even with patience and perseverance, retraining

a cat is not successful. If this proves to be the case, it may be necessary to prevent the cat from having unsupervised access to the home and confine it to one small room that is easily monitored.

GROOMING AND CARE

Grooming

Most cats are very clean and will groom themselves fastidiously as part of their daily routine, often upon waking after a sleep or following a meal. The cat does this by using its tongue, which has a roughened surface as a result of the presence of numerous minute, backward-pointing projections called papillae. The papillae collect loose hairs and particles of dust and dirt, and because they point backwards, the cat invariably swallows this material rather than spitting it out of its mouth. Hairs are effectively caught up on the papillae and are not easy to dislodge except by swallowing. If present in large quantities they may combine together to form fur balls or hair balls (*see* A-Z OF ILLNESSES, page 191) in the stomach, and these are especially likely to occur in long-haired cats. The most important reason for grooming a pet cat is to remove dead hair and to reduce the likelihood of the formation of fur balls.

A cat uses its tongue to lick and groom all the parts of its body that it can reach, wetting its fur with saliva as it does so. For the inaccessible places out of reach of its tongue, such as the head and ears, the cat licks its paw and cleans vigorously, rubbing until it is satisfied that no traces of dirt remain. A mother cat grooms her offspring in this way for the first three weeks of life, but kittens also soon begin to do this for themselves, becoming quite accomplished by about six weeks old. Kittens and cats also groom each other as part of their interactions with one another and as a means of cementing relationships.

A kitten or cat should be groomed regularly by its owner from the time it arrives in its new home, and both a comb and a brush are needed for this purpose. Short-haired types of cat need to be groomed once or twice a week and more often when they are moulting. Long-haired varieties need more frequent attention, but grooming is essential to prevent the formation of matted lumps of fur. A steel comb is the most suitable type to use and its teeth should be rounded to prevent scratching of the cat's skin.

It is best to start combing at the head and neck and to work gently down the body, teasing out tangles in the fur until the comb can be pulled through easily. Small sections of fur should be worked on each time, if the cat is a long-haired type, as otherwise there may be painful tugging on its skin. The tail should be included as well and also the fur on the underside. After being combed, the fur should be brushed to remove dislodged, dead hairs, and a brush with natural bristles is the most suitable kind to use. Suitable combs and brushes can be purchased at a pet shop at a fairly modest price. A final stroking with the hands or a glove or cloth will help to produce a shine on the coat and reward the cat if it has been well behaved during grooming.

It is all too easy for the fur of a long-haired cat to become impossibly tangled and matted. Breeds such as the Himalayan and Persian require a great deal of effort and attention if their coats are to be kept in good order. The situation is not helped by the fact that some cats strongly object to being combed and brushed, and it is necessary to be firm and to persevere. Usually, if regular grooming is started when the animal is a kitten, it learns to accept the procedure, and some really enjoy the process and the attention they receive. An adult cat that has not been accustomed to grooming may resent it and fight to get away. This can present considerable problems, especially with a long-haired cat that has a tangled coat. In these circumstances, it may be possible to brush the cat gently while it is being stroked and petted, and, all going well, it will learn to accept the procedure. A stronger approach is gently but firmly to grasp the cat by the scruff of its neck and to try to make sure that all its paws remain in contact with the surface on which it is placed while grooming is carried out.

If lumps of matted fur are found during grooming (usually in a long-haired cat), an attempt can be made to prise them apart with the fingers and then comb them through. If this is not pos-

sible, however, or the knots are large, they should be raised up
with the comb and cut off using round-ended scissors. A cat
with a severely tangled coat may need to have the knots
clipped off under general anaesthetic at a veterinary surgery.
Unfortunately, this situation tends to arise with cats that habitually bite, scratch and fight when any attempt is made to
groom them so that this is abandoned because it is too traumatic both for the animals and their owners.

Grooming provides an ideal opportunity to check the cat for
skin disorders, cuts or bites and fleas that may not be apparent
and can easily be overlooked at other times. At the same time,
the ears can be looked at to ensure that there are no signs of ear
mites and the eyes examined to ensure that they are bright and
clear. (*See also* PARASITES—External Parasites, pages 136,
140.)

Care of Teeth

Domestic pet cats are susceptible to the buildup of TARTAR, also
called dental calculus, on their teeth. Tartar deposits build up in
the presence of the growth of bacteria, plaque or accumula-
tions of trapped food and naturally occurring salts (mainly calcium hydroxyapatite) precipitated from the cat's saliva. This
buildup usually affects the canine teeth and also the premolars
and the first pair of molars in the upper jaw. It generally begins
to accumulate at the junction of the teeth with the gums as this

is the area that receives the least wear and exercise. Once tartar starts to accumulate, more material is deposited on its roughened surface until eventually the mass can be much greater than that of the tooth it is covering. At the same time, the gum becomes inflamed and irritated and pulls away from the base of the tooth, allowing a means of access for harmful bacteria. Bacterial infection in the root of the affected tooth, where it is set into the jaw, can ultimately be the result. The tooth may become loose and there may be an abscess beneath it, causing severe pain and bad breath (halitosis). This condition is called periodontal disease, and it is quite common in pet cats and dogs. (*See also* A-Z OF ILLNESSES, pages 150, 157, 206.)

In the wild, cats are constantly having to use their teeth to chew and eat their prey, and this continual exercise prevents the buildup of tartar. However, many domestic cats are fed almost exclusively on soft foods that can be swallowed without the teeth being involved at all. The best way to prevent the buildup of tartar on the teeth of a pet cat is to make sure that the animal eats some hard foods or is given toys and chews to bite on. It is possible to clean a cat's teeth gently using a special toothbrush that can be obtained from a veterinary clinic. (Alternatively, a baby's toothbrush can be used.) Toothpaste for human teeth should not be used although special preparations formulated for pets can be purchased. The cat needs to be placed on a table and held in a sitting position, by the scruff of the neck if necessary. The toothbrush should be gently inserted into the mouth and the teeth brushed with horizontal and vertical strokes. Brushing can help to prevent tartar buildup in a cat that is mainly fed on soft foods. Daily brushing is probably the most effective but even once or twice a week is helpful.

Ear and Eye Care

There is usually no need to clean the ears or eyes of a cat, which should normally be clear of signs of inflammation and infection. Inflammation of the ear caused by parasitic ear mites is quite common in cats and may result in severe irritation and self-inflicted damage by scratching. The most common sign of these mites is the presence of quantities of dark brown wax that forms flakes and crusts within the ear. A cat with any signs of ear or eye inflammation should be taken to a veterinary surgeon so that the appropriate diagnosis can be made and treatment given.

Worming

Responsible ownership involves regular dosing with medication designed to eliminate two types of internal parasite that are common in cats, roundworms and tapeworms (*see* PARASITES—Internal Parasites, pages 129, 132). A variety of deworming preparations are available in the form of tablets, syrups or creams. Some act solely on one type of worm while others combine preparations that will eliminate both. Particular vigilance is necessary to control roundworms in mother cats, before and after giving birth, and in kittens. It is wise to consult a veterinary surgeon, who will advise on the type of preparation needed and the frequency of use. In general, kittens are infected with only roundworms of a particular species (*Toxocara cati*), which they acquire as larvae from their mother's milk shortly after birth. Generally, it is only older cats that are allowed to go outside and mix with neighbouring pets and wildlife that are likely to acquire tapeworms. However, fleas are the intermediate hosts of the commonest tapeworm acquired by cats, *Dipylidium caninum*. Hence any cat in contact with fleas could be infested with tapeworms.

It is usually recommended that a pregnant cat should be treated for roundworms about one month before giving birth. Kittens should be treated every two weeks (for roundworms), beginning at three weeks of age, and this should continue until they are twelve weeks old. From twelve weeks to six months of age they should be wormed on a monthly basis. A cat that roams freely and hunts and kills prey should then be wormed three or four times each year with a preparation that will eliminate both roundworms and tapeworms. If a cat is kept indoors all the time, a less stringent routine may be needed of de-worming once or twice a year (*see* SEXUAL BEHAVIOUR AND BREEDING— Routine Care of a Queen and Her Kittens, page 115).

Vaccination

It is vitally important to protect the health of a kitten or older cat by making sure it is vaccinated against certain serious viral diseases that can prove fatal in untreated animals. Routine vaccination provides protection against the following diseases:

Feline infectious enteritis (*FIE*) or *feline pantenkopenia* (*FPL*). A viral form of gastroenteritis, which can be fatal in many cases. Vaccination is by means of a course of injections, starting at the age of nine weeks.

Feline influenza (cat 'flu) or *feline respiratory disease*. A variety of vaccines are available but normally vaccination is by means of a course of injections, starting at the age of nine weeks. With both these conditions, booster vaccinations must be given on a yearly basis once the initial course has been completed.

Feline leukaemia virus (*FeLV*). A serious viral disease that attacks the lymphoid tissues and is responsible, in many cats, for the formation of malignant growths called lymphosarcomas. The virus causes disruption and damage to various body systems and leaves the cat vulnerable to other infections by reducing its immunity. Recently a vaccine has been developed, and cats can now be protected by means of an injection against this often fatal infection.

It is vitally important to consult a veterinary surgeon about vaccination as soon as possible after acquiring a kitten or cat, so that a pet can be protected against these common infectious illnesses. It is usually possible to arrange for the first vaccination injection and general health checkup to be carried out at the same time, giving a good opportunity for any other problems to be discussed. The viral diseases of cats are particularly prevalent in cat rescue shelters or other premises where large numbers of different animals are brought together. Unfortunately, it is sometimes the case that a kitten acquired from an animal shelter is incubating one of these illnesses, to which it has very little natural immunity. In these circumstances, therefore, an early visit to a veterinary clinic is even more important.

Neutering

As mentioned earlier, the vast majority of pet cats in Britain are 'mongrels' and there is a considerable problem posed by a large number of unwanted, stray or feral animals. It is a part of responsible ownership, therefore, to have a cat neutered (castration in the male and spaying in the female), since it is very difficult to prevent mating and breeding. Some people feel uneasy about having a pet neutered and subjecting it to an operation, so it is worthwhile to outline the advantages, to the cat as well as to its owner.

An intact male cat, or tom, will roam widely in search of females with which to mate and will fight with rival males for the privilege of doing so. A tom cat can receive nasty injuries in fights, as bites and wounds easily become infected and abscesses can develop. It is not unusual for a tom cat to be absent from home for days on end and to return home thin, bedraggled, hurt and hungry, having caused a great deal of worry for his owners. Also, since a tom roams widely, it is much more likely to be killed or injured in a traffic accident. The lifestyle of a tom cat is stressful to the animal, and studies have shown that life expectancy is reduced compared to that of a castrated male. From an owner's point of view, a tom cat makes a much less agreeable pet, tending to be more aggressive, less affectionate and becoming associated with an unpleasant odour. The latter is related to the other major antisocial habit of a tom cat, that of spraying pungent urine to mark its territory, which includes the interior of the home.

Neutering is usually carried out before a kitten reaches puberty (around the age of seven to nine months) but after the testicles have entered the scrotum. It is normally a simple, untraumatic operation in the male, carried out under a general anaesthetic, and the cat quickly returns to normal within the space of a few hours. Castration usually prevents the development of the antisocial habits of a tom cat, particularly urine spraying and roaming. It is also highly effective in reducing this behaviour in older adult cats, although it may persist with individuals in whom sexual behaviour has become ingrained. (*See also* SEXUAL BEHAVIOUR AND BREEDING—Male Cat, page 92.)

A female cat reaches puberty around the age of six or seven months, marked by the first period of oestrus, or calling, when the animal is sexually receptive and willing to mate. Marked behavioural changes occur, the most significant one being that the cat develops a raucous loud 'call' to summon male cats in the neighbourhood. The cat is often restless and determined to get outside in order to be mated. Usually, neighbouring tom cats will gather in the garden or even on the doorstep of a home containing a calling female. Oestrus periods vary in length and are difficult to predict with any degree of accuracy. It is therefore very difficult to prevent a mating with an intact female cat. Even if their cat is normally kept indoors, owners have to be extremely vigilant in making sure that their pet does not slip outside unnoticed, and this is difficult to achieve. In order to ensure that a female cat will not become pregnant at all, she should be neutered or spayed before the age of six months. This is a straightforward abdominal operation carried out under a general anaesthetic and poses a minimal risk to the health of the cat.

Caring for the cat after the operation is very straightforward, and most animals are more or less back to normal by the following day. The female cat usually has a few stitches, which are removed seven to ten days later by the veterinary surgeon. Once again, it is worth remembering that producing endless litters of kittens, which is the fate that awaits most unneutered females, is stressful and takes its toll upon the health of the cat. Studies show that, on average, spayed female cats outlive those that habitually produce litters of kittens by two to three years. (*See also* SEXUAL BEHAVIOUR AND BREEDING—Female Cat, page 94 and A-Z OF ILLNESSES, page 203.)

Leaving a Cat at Home or in a Cattery

Some owners worry considerably about how their cat will adjust if it has to be left with other people while they are away. Cats are usually most secure in their own familiar home surroundings. The ideal situation from the cat's point of view, is if a relative or friend is able to come and stay in the house while the owners are away. The cat then has the benefit of human company and attention as well as its meals being given at the usual times, and generally it manages very well without its owners. More often that not, however, this is not possible and the best that can be managed is to arrange for someone to come in and feed the cat, let it in and out and check on its wellbeing. This may work quite well, particularly if the carer is able to come in and out quite frequently and to give the cat plenty of attention. Unfortunately, however, many cats hate it when their home is deserted and some may even wander away. For peace of mind, it may be better to arrange for the cat to be boarded at a cattery where one can be sure of its safety.

In most areas of the UK, there are plenty of catteries available. Many are boarding kennels for both dogs and cats while others cater exclusively for cats. It is often helpful to ask around and see if one in your area is particularly recommended or to seek advice from the local veterinary practice. Naturally, it is a good idea to visit the cattery yourself, well in advance of your departure, so that you can form an opinion as to how well run the premises are. All reputable catteries will welcome and even expect such a visit, which also gives an opportunity to discuss any particular needs of your cat. In the end, it is a matter of trusting your own judgement—if you like the look of the place and the owners then you will feel happier about leaving your cat in their care.

There are, however, a few points to look out for during an inspection visit. The cattery should appear to be clean, tidy and efficiently managed, with the accommodation for cats kept separate from any kennels for dogs. The accommodation for each cat should consist of a warm, enclosed indoor pen along with an attached exercise run. Alternatively, there should be a safely enclosed exercise pen where each cat is allowed to spend some time every day. The pens, runs, beds, feeding and water bowls, litter trays, etc, provided for the cats must be clean and hygienic. In winter it is important to make sure that indoor pens are adequately heated, and good ventilation is necessary, especially in hot, sunny weather. In a well-run cattery the people in charge will be obviously interested in the welfare of their charges and enthusiastic about cats. They should be happy to cater for reasonable individual requests, for instance food preferences, and to encourage the owner to bring the cat's favourite blanket or toy so that it will feel more at home. It should also be appreciated that one of the things most feared by proprietors is an outbreak of some infectious illness in their cattery. Hence, almost invariably, they will insist that each cat left with them has been vaccinated against the common feline diseases and will wish to see the proof of this in the form of an up-to-date vaccination certificate. Naturally, in the event of some unforeseen illness arising while the cat is being boarded, one should ensure that appropriate veterinary care will be obtained. It is worth bearing in mind that reputable catteries become booked up very quickly in recognized holiday periods so it is necessary to make plans well in advance to be sure of securing a place.

It is often the owners who experience more anxiety about their pet than the cat itself. It has to be said, however, that some cats are very unhappy about being left in a cattery, particularly older animals that dislike change. If, on acquiring a cat, you know that you will need to use a cattery on a regular basis, it is best to introduce this quite early on, once the animal has settled down with you. Many cats learn to accept a stay in a cattery, even if they do not enjoy it very much, and will always be very pleased to return home. Some may fret a little or go off their food, but often proprietors will do their best to reassure an unhappy cat and to try to coax it to eat. Most cats will not come to any harm if they lose a little weight and will soon regain lost ground once they return home. However, if experience shows that a cat has been severely depressed and miserable during its stay in a cattery, it is only kind to make alternative arrangements in the future.

ADAPTATIONS OF THE CAT

All members of the cat family are true carnivores which have to hunt and kill prey animals in order to survive. They are capable of running at great speed in short bursts of intense activity while in pursuit of prey. Most cats are good climbers, using trees or rocks as lookout posts for stalking prey or to retreat to, and hide in, when threatened.

Cats' Eyes

The ancestors of domestic cats, and other wild cats of similar size, primarily prey on small rodents, and these animals tend to be most active at dusk and during the night. The eyes of the cat are adapted to perceive objects in dim light, which is an obvious advantage in hunting. Cats have large eyes and the pupils are able to dilate widely in poor light. This allows as much light as possible to enter and fall onto the sensitive layer, called the retina, at the back of the eye. The retina of mammals contains special receptor cells, called rods and cones. Rod cells are sensitive to light of low intensity because of the presence of a pigment called rhodopsin (visual purple). The pigment alters when stimulated by low intensity light rays, and this causes nerve impulses to be generated which are sent along the optic nerves to the brain where they are interpreted. Cone cells are stimulated by bright light and produce sharper images than rod cells. They are responsible for the detection of colour, containing pigments that alter at different wavelengths. Cats' eyes contain a high proportion of rod cells compared to cones, a ratio of 25 rods to each cone. Experiments have shown that the cone cells of the cat are sensitive only to blue and green and there is no perception of red. Cats, in common with many other mammals, have a layer called the *tapetum lucidum* behind the retina, which is stimulated for a second time producing an intensified image. The tapetum lucidum can be clearly seen if a light is shone into the eyes of a cat at night when they appear to glow a greenish-yellow colour—'cats' eyes'. Compared to human beings, cats have poorer daytime and colour vision. They are able to detect moving objects better than static ones. In poor light, however, the visual acuity of the cat greatly exceeds that of a person and, combined with its other keen senses, helps to make it a superbly efficient twilight hunter.

The Ears

Cats have relatively large, pricked and highly mobile ears, which can collect and deflect sound rays inwards towards the eardrum and the organs of hearing. Cats are able to detect sounds with higher frequency wavelengths in the ultrasonic

81

range up to about 65 KHz. However, noises with lower frequency wavelengths below 30 KHz are not able to be heard. Observation of a cat leaves one in no doubt as to the accuracy with which it can locate and identify sounds. Since cats hunt by stealth, crouching, prowling and finally pouncing upon their prey, it is a great advantage to be able to hear the slightest rustle in the grass and the high-pitched sounds made by their rodent prey.

Smell

Cats have an acute and highly developed sense of smell and, in common with many mammals, possess a special pair of small olfactory organs located near the roof of the mouth. The vomeronasal, or Jacobson's organs, contain cells that are sensitive to chemical odours and, when stimulated, transmit signals along nerve pathways to the brain where these can be identified and interpreted. Occasionally a cat can be seen 'snuffing' a scent and curling its lip as though in disgust. In fact, what the cat is doing is directing the air it is inhaling through the vomeronasal organs better to detect the chemical particles that it contains. The part of the brain concerned with the interpretation of odours is relatively large, showing the importance of this sense in the life of a cat. The animal uses its olfactory sense to detect and interpret the scent messages, or pheromones, left by other cats in the area. This means that cats have a means of chemical communication, used primarily to advertise their sexual status and, in the case of males, to mark their territory.

The Whiskers

Cats have a well-developed set of whiskers, growing mainly from the cheeks on either side of the nose. These are long, stiff, strong hairs, each associated with sense cells that are very sensitive to touch. The whiskers are used by the cat to 'feel' its surroundings and are particularly useful at night. They can be used to gain information about the dimensions of spaces or objects, to detect movement or vibration and in interactions with other cats and with people. Similar sensory hairs occur along the back of the front legs (the 'carpal hairs'), and these, along with its whiskers, provide a cat with a highly developed sense of touch.

Balance

Cats are agile and sure-footed climbers with a highly developed sense of balance. Their claws enable them to obtain a good grip while climbing and the tail is used as a counterbalance. The organs of balance are the fluid-filled, semicircular canals within the inner ear, from which information is continually conveyed to the brain and interpreted. The processing of all information relating to spatial position, nature of the surface on which the cat is climbing, visual data, etc, is very rapid.

Electrical signals are sent to appropriate groups of muscles so that a cat is able to move rapidly and keep its balance even in difficult circumstances. Of course, as is well known, cats do sometimes get into difficulties and have to be rescued from high places, being too afraid to attempt a descent. A cat may also sometimes misjudge the distance of a jump, or lose its balance for some other reason, and fall. If a fall occurs, a series of 'righting reflexes' rapidly come into play so that a cat usually lands in an upright position on its paws. This helps to lessen the risk of injury but cannot prevent it altogether, especially if the cat falls from a height onto a hard surface. However, cats are popularly believed to possess 'nine lives' and are well known for their remarkable escapes from tricky situations. The characteristics described above are mainly responsible for the supposed nine lives of a cat.

The Teeth

Cats possess the teeth of a true carnivore, adapted for killing prey and eating flesh and bones. In particular, the long, pointed canine teeth are well developed and are used to kill prey by biting through the back of the neck to sever the spinal cord. They are also formidable weapons if the cat becomes involved in a fight. The last premolars in the upper jaw and the first molars in the lower jaw are the largest teeth present and are called the 'carnassials'. These have cusps with sharp, cutting edges and work against one another in a scissor-like motion, being used for slicing off and chewing the flesh of the prey animal. The smallest teeth are the six incisors at the front of the jaw between the two canines. These are used for carrying prey (or young kittens by a mother cat) as well as for teasing out small strips of flesh.

Behaviour, 'Language' and Communication

Compared to some other mammals, cats appear to have a wide range of behaviour, involving both the whole body and the voice, with which to communicate with one another and with people. About sixteen different types of vocal sound have been identified in cats, from the enquiring miaow of a cat that wants food or to go outside to the loud raucous call of a female in season and the corresponding yowls of a male. Mother cats make a soft chirping sound to their young kittens in order to encourage them to suckle and, at the other end of the scale, an angry cat may voice its disapproval with loud, continuous growls, hissing and spitting. Purring is the unique sound made by cats to indicate pleasure, produced by the very rapid and continuous buildup and release of air pressure across the vocal cords. Purring is produced with the mouth closed and is a continuous sound that carries on while the animal breathes in and out. It arises in very young kittens at about one week old, which are able to purr while suckling. Kittens probably use purring to communicate a sense of wellbeing to their mother just as, conversely, cries indicate distress. A nursing mother cat often purrs while settling down to suckle her young. This indicates contentment and strengthens the maternal bond with the kittens, showing them that all is well. During suckling, the kittens knead the area around their mother's teats with their front paws, extending the claws as they do so. Along with purring, this behaviour persists into adult life. Many cats purr and knead while being stroked by their owners, using this to indicate their feeling of intense pleasure. An affectionate cat usually greets its owner by purring and rubbing its head, body and legs around and through the person's legs. In addition to expressing pleasure and affection, the cat is using scent glands that are present on the head, face and tail to mark the person as its own.

Body Language

In the cat, body language is a very important means of communication. An alert but relaxed cat walks along with its tail held high, possibly with the end bent forwards slightly, and the ears pricked up. When its owner approaches, it may lower its head and raise its rear quarters, holding the tail erect and rocking slightly before purring and rubbing against the person's legs as described above. The cat's behaviour expresses pleasure and anticipation in meeting its owner. Tail wagging that becomes steadily more pronounced is a means of expressing anger and is usually accompanied by growling. A cat that is frightened by the approach of another animal it perceives as a potential threat tenses its whole body and may be ready to run if necessary. The pupils of the eyes widen and the cat may crouch down, lower its tail and flatten its ears against its head, which are submissive gestures. If the encroaching stranger approaches too closely, however, the cat may arch its back, raise its body hair and stand sideways, accompanying these warning signs with growling, hissing and bared teeth. The tail is usually held erect and, while still alarmed, the cat is trying to communicate that it is not to be trifled with. This defensive behaviour combines elements of submission (widened pupils and flattened ears) with those of aggression (raised hackles, arched back, bared teeth and growling). If this approach does not deter the encroaching animal, the cat may spring into the attack, especially if it feels that it cannot escape.

In encounters with other cats, the behaviour displayed depends upon the circumstances and the individual temperament of each animal. If both animals are tom cats, each may adopt a determined and aggressive stance in order to establish which is dominant. Each cat tenses its body and stretches its head forward, with ears pricked and tail held stiffly horizontal or slightly lower than the line of its back. The tail waves slightly and each cat slowly and stiffly approaches the other with narrowed pupils, trying to stare out its opponent. These movements are accompanied by angry growling that rises and falls in intensity. During this 'standoff' period, tail-wagging and growling may increase until, if neither backs down, one cat eventually launches into attack. The weaker cat may eventually show submissive behaviour, crouching down and flattening its ears or running away in retreat.

Licking and grooming is another indication of mood in a cat. When excited or upset, the cat may lick itself with vigorous, quick movements in an almost obsessional manner, as if trying to shut out what is happening around it. This is a type of displacement activity that seems to help the cat to cope with whatever has caused its agitation as a means of calming it down. This type of licking is in marked contrast to the slow, luxurious grooming indulged in by a relaxed and contented cat that is at peace with itself and its surroundings.

Cats may change quite suddenly from submissive to defensive behaviour and this occasionally arises when an animal is being stroked and petted. A cat often lies half on its side and half on its back with the upper paw raised while being stroked. This is similar to the submissive posture adopted when trying to appease another potentially aggressive cat, but the raised paw is ready to strike if necessary. Usually, if stroking continues beyond a certain point, the cat suddenly becomes irritated and lashes out with its claws and teeth before leaping up and jumping away. It seems that the animal suddenly feels threatened and the stroking is no longer welcome, as though the attention is coming from another cat. Usually, before the moment of attack is reached, the cat gives warning signs such as flicking its tail and possibly growling. It is wise to be wary when stroking a cat in this position and to avoid continuing for too long, as this behaviour is common and can be quite painful for the person concerned!

Hunting Behaviour

The hunting instinct is strongly developed in all members of the cat family, and the act of stalking and killing prey is arguably the most important activity in their daily life. Domestic cats, even after thousands of years of association with human beings and having food regularly provided for them, retain the strong instinct to hunt and kill. Although their natural prey is small rodents, cats also hunt birds, fish out of garden ponds, frogs, squirrels, young rabbits and even insects such as bluebottles and butterflies. Like most members of the cat family, cats hunt by stealth, relying on a final burst of speed actually to catch and dispatch the prey animal. The cat crouches low in the grass, watching its prey intently with narrowed pupils and ears pricked, displaying great concentration. The whole body is tense, and before making a final spring the cat raises itself and may rock slightly and lash its tail before pouncing. The animal is caught with the front paws, claws and teeth. As is well known, however, in many instances a cat does not kill its prey outright but spends some time apparently tormenting and playing with the animal before finally finishing it off. It is this aspect of behaviour that many people find extremely distressing and abhor the apparent cruelty of the cat. It is a mistake to seek to endow animals with human motives and feelings, and one explanation for this behaviour is that it is a means of dealing with nervous energy following a capture. It is also the case that a mother cat brings live prey to her kittens when they are between six and ten weeks old so that they can learn how to pounce and kill. They also accompany their mother and learn how to hunt by watching her. Playing with prey may be behaviour that persists into adult life, reflecting these earlier experiences. Kittens born to a mother cat that does not hunt or bring back live prey are much less likely to become adept hunters themselves. Cats often present their catch to their owner, bringing it back for inspection. This would seem to be a throwback to the days of kittenhood when a mother cat brought home live prey to teach her family how to hunt. It has to be said that it is their hunting skill that enables pet cats to survive on their own if the need arises.

A well-fed pet cat certainly does not need to hunt to survive. It is perfectly in order to try to discourage hunting, for instance by fitting the cat with a collar and a bell.

Sexual Behaviour and Breeding

Male Cat

Male cats generally reach puberty and become sexually active between nine and twelve months of age, although there is a great deal of variation in this and in some it can be as early as seven months. Once puberty is reached, a tom cat can mate at any time with a sexually receptive female and there is no breeding season for males. A pedigree stud tom cat is not usually used for breeding until he is one year old, and the number of matings in the first year should be limited to about five. He can continue to mate throughout his life but is usually 'retired' by the age of about six years.

As mentioned previously, once a tom cat reaches puberty, he sprays a pungent-smelling urine at suitable points to mark his territory and advertise his presence. During the breeding season, when there are females in the area ready to mate, urine spraying is performed even more frequently. The urine contains chemical substances, known as pheromones, that are attractive to sexually receptive female cats. When a female cat is calling and advertising her willingness to mate, all the tom cats within range are attracted to her. The tom cats fight fiercely for the privilege of mating although it is the watching female who chooses which tom she will accept. Neutered males (*see* GROOMING AND CARE—Neutering, page 73) may be attracted to watch the proceedings and can be drawn into fights under these circumstances. Any cat can be involved in an occasional fight. Roaming tom cats, however, are more likely to receive injuries in battles with rivals and usually become scarred over the years as a result of these frequent encounters.

Of course, in the breeding of pedigree cats, matings can be planned and the whole process made more civilized for the stud tom as rivals are eliminated. A stud tom cat is usually housed in suitable accommodation outside the home. This should consist of a spacious outdoor run containing a tree branch, shelves and other vantage points to which the cat can climb and bask in the sun. The floor should be concrete as this can be easily washed and disinfected. The cat should have access to a warm 'house' or shed that contains his bed and perhaps some other home comforts and toys. Tom cats, especially if kept in confined quarters, are liable to develop a condition known as 'stud tail'. This is an accumulation of greasy, crusted material along the length of the tail that must be treated by washing with a suitable solution and thorough grooming (*see* GROOMING AND CARE, page 65). Usually there are separate adjacent runs and houses in which visiting or resident female ('queen') cats are accommodated. A tom cat is happier if he has plenty of human company and establishes a good, affectionate relationship with his owners. He should therefore be allowed out into the garden and house from time to time and be treated as a pet as well as a valuable breeding animal. Reputable, caring breeders are naturally likely to do this as a matter of course, as the ultimate aim is to win prizes at shows with their cats. Hence each animal is a treasured individual that is well used to the grooming, pampering and attention that is such a prominent part of the cat show.

Female Cat or Queen

Most female kittens reach puberty around the age of six to ten months old, although there is considerable variation in this. For instance, a feral cat that reaches the right age in the cold winter months may not become sexually active until the weather is warmer in the spring. At puberty, the female becomes sexually active and willing, and able to mate and produce kittens. This is popularly known as being 'in season', 'on heat' or 'calling' but is scientifically designated as being in 'oestrus'. In female cats there is a breeding season during which most matings take place. This period extends from January to September but with two peaks of activity (at the beginning and end of the season) during which the oestrus cycles are more obvious. During the autumn and winter months, when daylight hours are short, most female cats enter an anoestrus phase when cycles cease. This is not at all predictable, however, and some females may continue to have cycles even although they may be less frequent than at other times. A female is capable of reproducing before she has finished growing herself. This is highly detrimental to the young cat and her growth is likely to suffer as a consequence. This is because the young cat is simply not able to take in enough food to allow for her own growth and that of the rapidly developing kittens. Even if she is fed very well, the young mother will probably always remain small and not achieve her full size, although she may make up some lost ground once her kittens are weaned. It is necessary therefore to prevent a young queen from mating, which either means keeping her confined or giving her synthetic hormone treatment to suppress her oestrus cycles. This treatment must be prescribed by a veterinary surgeon and the hormones (called progestogens) are given either in tablet form or as an injection. Of course, if the female is a non-pedigree, mongrel cat, the most satisfactory option is to have her neutered or spayed by the age of six months. Hormone treatment is a useful means of delaying oestrus cycles in a young pedigree female cat so that a planned mating can take place when she is fully mature. Its main advantage is that owners are relieved of the nuisance of calling, which can be quite loud and persistent, and the necessity of keeping the cat confined. It is generally accepted that a queen should not have her first litter of kittens until she is at least ten months of age or preferably one year old. If hormonal treatment has been given, the cat's body needs time to adjust once the drugs have been withdrawn. Usually the first oestrus cycle occurs about three months after drug treatment is halted, and most breeders prefer to wait for the next one before allowing the cat to mate.

Oestrus usually lasts from one to three days but can be as long as ten days. If the cat does not mate, another cycle generally begins after two weeks, but this is variable. In some cats, cycles seem to follow rapidly and unpredictably if the animal is prevented from mating. These animals may develop ovarian cysts, which can cause infertility because of disruption of the balance of hormones. During the period leading up to oestrus, the behaviour of the female usually changes. She frequently becomes more affectionate than usual, insisting upon being petted and rolling on her back. She will then become increasingly restless, watching for her chance to get outside in search of a mate and starting to 'call', using her voice in an unusual way. Calling sounds vary from one cat to another but tend to be loud and raucous and almost like a howl at times. Siamese cats are especially vocal in this respect, perhaps because they are one of the most 'talkative' breeds of cat. The vulva, which is the external opening of the genital tract, becomes enlarged at this time, although this is not usually noticed. There may also be slight mucus discharge, but this is cleaned away by the cat during grooming and is unlikely to be detected.

If a calling queen is allowed to roam freely, she will almost certainly mate repeatedly with several of the neighbourhood tom cats, which fight each other to gain access to her. Ovulation, or the release of eggs, occurs in response to mating in cats so that it is possible for a litter of kittens to have more than one father. This is known as 'superfecundation' and is probably quite a common occurrence. The behaviour associated with oestrus declines quite rapidly once the cat has mated, and the episode almost invariably results in pregnancy. It is possible to prevent a pregnancy from taking place, however, by giving an injection of oestrogen hormone. This must be administered by a veterinary surgeon within forty hours of mating and prevents the fertilized eggs from developing in the normal way. This procedure is usually carried out with a pedigree queen cat that has inadvertently got out while calling.

Owners need to make preparations if they plan to breed kittens from a pedigree queen cat. The usual procedure, once a suitable stud tom cat has been found, is to arrange for the female to go to him at the start of her calling period. The tom and queen are usually placed in adjacent accommodation at first so that they can be introduced to each other through a wire mesh screen. Generally, after one or two days and ideally on the second day of the queen's period of oestrus, the two cats are allowed in together. Once they have got used to each other, and if the queen is prepared to accept the tom, mating usually takes place. It is best if at least two or more observed matings take place to increase the chances of a pregnancy. As stated above, the oestrus period usually declines quite quickly after a queen has been mated. As a precaution, however, it is best to restrict the queen's freedom for a few more days to make absolutely sure that she does not subsequently mate with a mongrel tom. Occasionally a queen cat may be so disturbed by being plucked from her familiar surroundings that her oestrus symptoms subside and she refuses to accept the stud tom. The mating may also, for some other reason, be unsuccessful and fail to result in pregnancy. Usually the owner of the tom cat will allow another free visit by the queen at a future date in order to try to remedy the situation.

There may be quite a lot of noisy interaction between the two partners before the actual mating takes place. When indicating that she is ready to mate, the queen lowers the front end of her body but raises her hindquarters and holds her tail on one side. The tom cat stands astride the queen with his legs placed on either side and seizes the back of her neck with his teeth before beginning to mate. The penis of a tom cat is covered with backward pointing barbed hairs, and the movement of these during mating is believed to stimulate the ejaculation of semen containing sperm. They are also believed to play a part in stimulating ovulation in the queen cat. The hairs, or papillae, degenerate in a neutered male cat that is not involved in mating. In some, but not all, adult tom cats a small bone develops inside the penis that gives additional strength during mating. The bone, called the os penis, is only $1/2$ cm in length and is formed from a gradual conversion (or ossification) of tissue within the penis into bone. The os penis is present as a much more definite structure in all male dogs. This may be connected with the fact that the mating process in dogs is a much more prolonged affair than in cats so the additional strengthening is advantageous. It would appear that the bone is not essential for reproductive success in cats but may confer an advantage to the animals in which it is developed. Mating is quite a brief process, and the animals soon separate and may then spend some time grooming. Some queen cats are quite aggressive after mating and may turn on the tom, using teeth, claws, spitting and growling to chase him away.

Pseudopregnancy

Occasionally following oestrus a queen that has not been mated nevertheless develops signs of pregnancy. There may be physical signs, such as the enlargement of the abdomen, even although there are no embryos growing in the womb, and swelling of the mammary glands and teats with the production of milk. Eventually the cat may search out a suitable corner and scratch around to make a bed in the typical manner of a female in the final stages of pregnancy. Usually the physical and behavioural changes gradually subside and the cat returns to normal. Pseudo, false or phantom pregnancy is much rarer in cats than in dogs, although it can be artificially induced by human interference. The procedure is generally carried out to halt oestrus, particularly the nuisance of calling which has been continuing for some time. Mating is simulated using a lubricated sterile glass pipe or cotton bud, which is gently inserted into the cat's vagina and carefully moved forwards and backwards and from side to side. A second person holds the cat firmly by the back of the neck, as would be the case if she was genuinely being mated. The effect of this is to stimulate ovulation to take place and hence the rapid cessation of oestrus. Pseudopregnancy follows in the manner previously described, but there is no fertilization of eggs or implantation and development of embryos. Some breeders of pedigree cats employ a vasectomized male, which has previously been used as a stud tom and continues to be capable of mating, for the same purpose.

Pseudopregnancy usually lasts for about five to six weeks after which the queen eventually resumes calling. Obviously, inducing ovulation and pseudopregnancy are useful in helping a breeder to plan and space out the litters of kittens produced by a particular queen. It may be less traumatic for the cat than the frustration of continual calling when she is not permitted to mate.

Pregnancy

The normal outcome of mating is ovulation, fertilization of the released eggs by the sperm of one or more tom cats, implantation of the embryos in the womb and pregnancy. The eggs are released from the ovaries and fertilized high up in the oviducts (equivalent to the human Fallopian tubes). The oviducts are a pair of narrow tubes that connect each ovary with the womb. The eggs travel down the ducts and become attached inside the womb or uterus, which is roughly Y-shaped, having a short 'body' and two longer 'arms' or 'horns'. The eggs or embryos become lodged at regular intervals along each horn of the uterus and eventually become attached to its lining. A placenta develops to nourish each foetus and to remove waste products. Oxygen and nutrients pass from the blood of the mother cat via the placenta to the developing foetus, and waste products pass the other way. All the mother's blood is filtered and cleaned by her kidneys and waste products are eliminated in urine. The mother cat's blood, and that of each developing foetus, remains entirely separate. Each foetus develops into a fully formed kitten within a fluid-filled membrane or amniotic sac and is attached to its placenta by an umbilical cord.

The usual length of pregnancy, or the gestation period, is 63 to 65 days in cats. There is a degree of variation between individuals, however, and kittens may arrive a few days before or after the expected time. Pregnancy can be difficult to diagnose with certainty in its early stages. A common sign about three weeks after conception is a deepening in the colour of the nipples, which become a definite pink and possibly slightly enlarged. At about four to five weeks, an experienced person is able to feel the foetuses within the abdomen. At this stage, they feel rather like small, round pebbles but may easily be damaged by inexpert handling. From six weeks onwards, the foetuses grow very rapidly, and the cat's abdomen starts visibly to increase in size. During the final stages of pregnancy, from about seven to nine weeks, it may be possible to see the kittens moving, especially when the mother cat is relaxed and lying still.

A small proportion of pregnant female cats (about 10 per cent) continue to have oestrus cycles and may call every three weeks. This is because of a deficiency in the hormone progesterone, which is produced during pregnancy and normally inhibits oestrus cycles at this time. If the cat is allowed to roam, it is possible for her to mate, ovulate and for the eggs to be fertilized and implanted in the normal way. In this situation, the cat is pregnant with two sets of foetuses at different stages of maturity—a condition known as 'superfoetation'. When this arises, the cat goes into labour when the first set of kittens are ready to be born. The immature foetuses are usually expelled at the same time and are frequently dead or do not survive. Rarely, the second set of foetuses are retained and are born alive at the appropriate time.

For the first six weeks a pregnant cat should continue to receive her normal ration of food, and there is no need to add vitamin or mineral supplements as long as she is eating a good, balanced diet. When the foetuses have entered the stage of rapid growth, during the last month of pregnancy, the mother cat's appetite increases. She should be offered a correspondingly increased amount of food as a separate meal. The quantity should be gradually increased until she is being offered up to half or even twice as much as usual. The food should always be divided and given as several small meals throughout the day so that there is less discomfort from a swollen uterus pressing on an overloaded stomach. Also, if she is fed a little and often, the level of nutrients and energy supply is maintained at a more constant level.

There is no need to try to limit the activities of the mother cat. Exercise is good for her in the early stages of pregnancy in keeping muscles well toned. In the final month, her increased weight and abdominal distension will normally stop the expectant mother from attempting any over-vigorous manoeuvres. Great care should be exercised throughout the pregnancy in handling, and especially in lifting, the mother cat. She should always be lifted with one hand under her 'armpits' (ax-illae) and the other supporting the weight beneath her rear quarters and tail. The cat can be then held in an upright position supported against the person's chest. In this way, no pressure is exerted on the abdomen of the cat.

Preparing for the Birth of Kittens

The most important preparation to be made is to provide the cat with a warm, comfortable and quiet place in which to give birth to her kittens. This should be introduced when it is no-ticed, usually during the last two or three weeks, that the cat is becoming restless and obviously searching for a suitable place to make a 'nest'. An ideal 'kittening' box is a large, strong, cardboard box, with the sides measuring about 60 to 80 centi-metres. The flaps that form the top of the box should be taped together with parcel tape, and one of the sides cut round on three sides to form a hinged lid. This then becomes the top of the box. At the front, a square of cardboard should be cut out and removed to form an entry hole for the cat. The lower edge of this should be about 15 centimetres above the base of the box so that the kittens cannot accidentally fall out when they are small.

The base of the box should be lined with layers of newspaper which the cat will scratch and tear to make a nest. Newspaper has the advantage that it can easily be removed and replaced if it should become wet or soiled during or after birth. It is safer not to add a blanket at first as it is possible for tiny kittens to become trapped if it becomes wrinkled or folded.

The box should be placed in a warm quiet corner away from the noise of family activity as the cat needs security and privacy. A litter tray should be placed near the box. It is to be hoped that the cat will accept the box as a suitable place to have her kittens. It has to be said, however, that a cat can have her own ideas about a nesting place and may select somewhere

A simple 'kittening' box

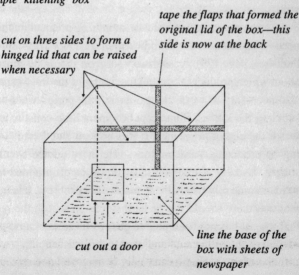

tape the flaps that formed the original lid of the box—this side is now at the back

cut on three sides to form a hinged lid that can be raised when necessary

cut out a door

line the base of the box with sheets of newspaper

entirely different. It is also a natural part of a cat's behaviour to have more than one potential site and to make the final choice when labour is about to start. This can be a place outside in a garden shed or garage, and many a mother cat has returned home after a period of absence, slim and hungry, having obviously had her kittens elsewhere. She may then bring them to the house, laboriously carrying each one by the scruff of the neck. It is preferable to keep the cat confined in the last days of her pregnancy, using her box and litter tray, but this may not be possible with a very independent cat that is used to roaming at will.

At some stage during the last month of pregnancy, the cat needs to be treated for roundworms (*see* PARASITES—Internal Parasites, page 129). A veterinary surgeon should be consulted about which product to use and the timing of the treatment. It is also necessary to worm the cat during the period when she is suckling the kittens. Some cats become a little constipated towards the end of pregnancy. If it is noticed that a cat is straining or producing hard motions, veterinary advice should be sought. Usually a teaspoonful of liquid paraffin added to the food or some oily fish helps to resolve the problem. It is important that there should not be hard stools present in the rectum that the cat has not been able to pass as these can cause a narrowing of the birth canal and a more difficult labour.

If the cat is a long-haired one, it may be advisable to cut

away the fur around her nipples and vulva using round-ended scissors. It is better not to do this, however, if the cat objects or becomes upset.

The majority of cats accomplish the process of birth very well on their own and do not require human assistance. It may be advisable, however, to have one or two items prepared and at hand in case intervention is necessary. These include:

1 Setting aside one or two small clean towels in case a kitten has to be handled and dried following its birth;

2 Having ready a pair of scissors and some strong sewing thread, which have been sterilized by boiling or immersion in a proprietary solution. Rarely, these may be needed for tying off and cutting an umbilical cord;

3 Setting aside a hot-water bottle with a good protective fitted cover. A kitten can be placed on or near a warm hot-water bottle if there are any difficulties while other kittens are being born.

These items should be placed in a convenient space close to the kittening box so that it is not necessary to search for them, perhaps in the middle of the night. In the great majority of cases these precautions will not prove to be necessary.

Labour and Birth

During the hours leading up to the onset of labour, the cat is often quite restless, going into and out of the kittening box, re-arranging and kneading the bedding and sometimes purring. She may go off her food and visit the litter tray several times although little is passed. As she enters the first stage of labour, the body temperature drops slightly by 1°C to 37.5°C and there may be a slight, clear discharge from the vulva. As the second stage of labour approaches, the cat may begin panting and purring and occasionally miaowing. During the true second stage of labour, there are strong abdominal contractions with straining, as the first kitten moves down through the birth canal. The cat licks the entrance to the vagina (vulva) repeatedly and may cry out and appear distressed. The queen is often comforted if the owner is stroking and talking to her at this time. Most cats lie on one side while giving birth but may stand and squat if straining particularly hard. Generally the first kitten arrives within 30 minutes of the onset of the second stage of labour. The kitten is surrounded by the fluid-filled membranes of the amniotic sac and often these rupture during the passage down the birth canal so that its birth is preceded by a gush of transparent fluid. Sometimes the sac is still intact when the presenting part of the kitten appears at the vulva. The mother cat is vigorously licking herself at this time and usually severs the membrane in the process. Occasionally the kitten is born still within the sac and its fluid, appearing to be encased, in a dull grey balloon. Once again, firm licking by the mother's rough tongue severs the membrane and releases the fluid. The mother cat continues to lick the kitten, and this stimulates it to breathe on its own, which is indicated by mewing sounds. She also bites through the umbilical cord, which at this stage is still attached to the placenta, or afterbirth, inside her body. While licking the kitten, the mother cat also eats the surrounding membranes. Most kittens are born head first (about 66 per cent), with the remainder in the breech position, i.e. the tail and hind end with the back legs tucked forwards beneath the body. The birth of a kitten in the breech position may take longer than normal, and there is a greater risk of stillbirth. Once the kitten has been born, contractions begin again after about five minutes or longer, marking the third stage of labour in which the placenta, or afterbirth, is expelled. This usually occurs quite easily and quickly, and the afterbirth is a dark brown colour, looking rather like a piece of liver. Some brownish discoloured liquid may also be discharged at the same time, and it is normal for the mother to eat the placenta, which is believed to contain hormones that may promote milk production. In the wild the placenta is probably eaten along with the membranes, to conceal the evidence of a birth from potential predators. It may also provide the mother with much needed nourishment in the immediate aftermath of birth, when the cat is not able to leave the kittens to go and hunt. In the domestic situation it is probably better if the owner can remove the afterbirth and dispose of it by burning. If the cat eats too many of them, it may make her sick.

The time taken for all the kittens to be born varies considerably but usually it is between one and three hours. A longer time is not abnormal, however, and in some cats there is a natural delay after the birth of the first one or two kittens. The rest of the litter may not follow for a further twelve hours or even longer in some cases. Usually there is a brief respite between each kitten when contractions cease, giving the mother time to lick the new arrival and nudge it towards her nipples. It is also not uncommon for the kittens to be born in quick succession and the afterbirths to be expelled at a later stage. It is essential that all the placentas are passed because if one is left behind it is likely to cause infection and illness, which can be life-threatening. Obviously, it is only possible to be sure about this if the births are observed from the beginning. However, a mother cat should be closely monitored in the succeeding hours to make sure that she appears to be well.

Once all the kittens have been born and are washed to their mother's satisfaction, they crawl towards her teats and start to suckle. Some mother cats suckle the first arrivals before the rest of the litter are born but others wait until birth is completed before settling down with the whole family. Most kittens are feeding within one or two hours of birth, and it is essential that suckling begins within twelve hours if each is to survive. The cat should be offered a drink of milk or water in her bed, once she has settled down with her new family. Food can also be offered although it may be refused, especially if the placentas have been eaten. It may be possible to remove newspaper that is soiled, but only if this can be accomplished without causing undue disturbance.

When to Intervene or Call a Vet

In the majority of births the queen cat manages perfectly well on her own. If it is evident that all is proceeding smoothly, she should be left in peace but kept under unobtrusive observation, or given gentle reassurance if this seems to be helpful. There are occasions, however, when it may be necessary to give some assistance or to call for expert veterinary help. An owner should intervene in the following circumstances:

1 The kitten is in one of the two common birth positions and is partly delivered but is stuck and is not being pushed out by subsequent contractions. The person should wash his or her hands thoroughly and then gently grasp the exposed part of the kitten through a layer of clean towel. The body should be pushed back a little (about one centimetre) and then turned slightly. With the next contraction, the kitten should then be

111

pulled gently outwards. Rather than one straight movement, it may help to pull a little to one side and then to the other with each contraction, taking care not to exert undue force.

2 The kitten is born still enclosed in its fluid-filled amniotic membrane and the cat fails to bite through this and the umbilical cord. The person should wash his or her hands thoroughly before puncturing the membrane with fingers or a sterile pair of scissors, close to the kitten's mouth to enable it to breathe. The membranes should be gently pulled from the body and removed. The umbilical cord should be tied with sterile thread about five centimetres from the kitten's body and then cut on the outer side of the knot. The kitten should then be rubbed dry with a towel, and this should stimulate breathing if this has not happened already. Particular attention should be paid to the area around the nose and mouth in order to remove any membrane or fluid. The kitten may also be swung gently up and down while being safely held enclosed by the hands as this helps to clear the respiratory passages.

3 A kitten is born apparently lifeless and fails to start breathing. If the licking of the mother cat has failed to stimulate the kitten to breathe there is probably little that can be done. As a last resort, the kitten can be wrapped in a towel and

swung gently up and down, while held in the hands, to remove any fluid that might be hindering breathing. The person may then gently blow into the kitten's nostrils in a final attempt to encourage it to breathe. A revived kitten should immediately be returned to its mother.

Emergency veterinary assistance must be obtained if any of the following circumstances arise:

1 The queen cat has been straining and having powerful contractions for an hour without any sign of a kitten appearing. In this case it is likely that a kitten is lying in an awkward, transverse position and has become stuck in the birth canal or a kitten may be abnormal or deformed or simply too large. Occasionally, two kittens may have started to descend the birth canal together and become stuck. Sometimes a kitten may become stuck because of an undiagnosed problem in the mother cat, usually an abnormality of the pelvis.

2 Labour has started normally and one or two kittens may already have been born when contractions become weaker and possibly stop altogether before the remainder are delivered. This conditions is known as 'uterine inertia', and an injection to restart contractions may be required or the kittens may need to be delivered by Caesarean section (*see* A-Z OF ILLNESSES, page 161).

3 A kitten is stuck partly inside and partly outside the mother's body and the owner's attempt to dislodge it has failed.

In all three circumstances, a likely outcome is that the kittens will need to be delivered by emergency Caesarean section carried out under a general anaesthetic. The veterinary surgeon may suggest that the cat is immediately brought to the premises so that the operation can be carried out under optimum conditions.

4 There is any suspicion that a placenta has not been expelled. It is far better for this to be diagnosed early and for appropriate action to be taken as there is a considerable risk of a serious infection arising. Treatment may involve giving drugs, including antibiotics, and surgery.

Veterinary advice and attention is advisable if any assistance has been necessary during the birth, particularly if there are any worries about the health of the kittens. Sometimes kittens are born with congenital abnormalities that make it unlikely that they will survive. A kitten that cries a lot and seems unable to suckle may have such a condition, and it is kinder to have it humanely put to sleep.

The mother cat should be observed closely in the period following birth to make sure that she is well. If she seems at all listless, is uninterested in her kittens or in food and is generally off colour, then she should be seen by a veterinary surgeon as soon as possible. If there is any sign of a foul-smelling or excessive vaginal discharge either before or after birth then this is indicative of an infection that must be treated immediately. Before birth, a possible cause is a foetus that has died and started to deteriorate within the uterus. Following birth, a likely cause is either a retained dead foetus or a placenta that has not been expelled. These conditions threaten the life of the mother cat and must be treated as a matter of urgency. The cat is likely to need a course of antibiotics and may require surgery. A slight, red-stained discharge from the vagina is quite normal in a queen cat for about two to three weeks after birth, and she will clean this away herself. As long as it does not smell and is not excessive, there is no cause for concern. If, however, at any time during pregnancy or after birth there is actual bleeding, the cat should receive immediate veterinary attention.

Routine Care of a Queen Cat and Her Kittens

If, as is usually the case, the birth has proceeded normally, it is to be hoped that there will be little for the owner to do during the first three weeks of the kittens' lives. Most queens are very good and attentive mothers and take care of all their kittens' needs during this initial period. In the early days, the kittens divide their time between periods of feeding and sleeping. It is especially important that they receive the first milk, or colostrum, that is produced during the 48 hours following birth. It contains vital antibodies that help to protect the kittens from infections and transferred only at this time. The degree of protection afforded and the length of time that it lasts depends upon the amount of colostrum each kitten consumes and the amount of antibodies it contains. The latter depends upon the immunity status of the mother cat. Some veterinary surgeons recommend giving a mother cat a booster vaccination during the last month of pregnancy to increase antibody levels. In this case, 'dead' inert vaccine is used, which stimulates the production of antibodies by the mother's immune system but poses no risk to developing foetuses.

Newborn kittens are blind and seem weak and helpless and yet are 'programmed' to crawl towards their mother's teats and to suckle. In any litter, but especially in a large one, there are usually one or two kittens that are smaller and weaker than the rest. Often, first-born kittens are slightly bigger and soon become dominant, establishing a claim on the most productive nipple, while weaker individuals can be pushed out and have to make do with one that produces less milk. Hence it can be hard for a smaller kitten to overcome an early disadvantage, and if there are deaths in the early days it is usually because of malnutrition. It is worth remembering that the queen's rear teats, nearest to her hind legs, produce the greater quantity of milk.

After only two or three days, the strongest and most dominant kittens will have established a claim upon them. If the mother cat accepts the interference, it is acceptable to intervene gently and swap two kittens round so that a weaker one occasionally obtains a turn at a richer feeding station. Occasionally a mother cat fails to produce enough milk to feed her kittens adequately. An indication of this is when the kittens cry continuously and fail to gain weight. They should gain about 10 to 15 grams each day or 80 to 100 grams every week. If signs of poor nourishment are present, a veterinary surgeon should be consulted about supplementary feeding (*see* Rearing Orphan Kittens, page 121).

During the first 48 hours, which coincides with the time when the colostrum is being passed, many cats are reluctant to leave their kittens at all. It is best to try to persuade the queen to do so in order that she can have food, drink and an opportunity to use the litter tray. This also allows time to change the newspaper in the bed.

The mother cat spends a great deal of time in the early weeks licking and grooming each kitten thoroughly. By licking beneath the tail she both stimulates the passage of waste and keeps this area clean. There is a great deal of communication between the queen and her kittens, with 'chirruping', mewing and purring. The kittens are particularly vocal when their mother is absent or returns to the bed after a short time away.

They crawl over one another and generally jostle for the best feeding position until settling down contentedly to suckle.

The queen cat should be observed for any signs of mastitis (*see* A-Z OF ILLNESSES, page 202). This usually affects only some of the milk glands and is an infection that causes swelling, heat and pain. The area around the affected teats feels hard and looks red and is so painful that the cat does not permit suckling and feels ill and miserable. Obviously, it is best if this is detected at an early stage and prompt veterinary treatment is obtained. Generally, the cat is given a course of antibiotics, which brings rapid relief of the symptoms. It may be necessary to give the kittens some supplementary feeding until the symptoms subside. A much rarer condition is eclampsia, or 'milk fever' (*see* A-Z OF ILLNESSES, page 175), which is brought about by a lack of calcium in the blood. The cat is evidently ill, shows no interest in her kittens and trembles or staggers. Emergency veterinary treatment is needed in the form of a calcium injection, which brings a rapid reversal of the symptoms. If treatment is not given, however, the condition can progress to a fatal outcome. Symptoms are a soaring temperature, convulsions, muscle spasms, coma and death. Eclampsia is a much rarer condition in cats than in dogs, and when it does occur it usually affects queens with large litters of at least five kittens. The most usual time for it to appear is two to four weeks after birth.

For the first three to four weeks, while the queen is feeding her rapidly growing kittens, her nutritional demands are enormous and it is difficult to overfeed her at this time. It is best to offer at least three good quality balanced meals a day and more if necessary. The cat should also be offered a constant supply of fresh water as she needs to replenish the fluid continually being lost in milk production. Milk provides an additional valuable source of protein and calcium and should be offered each day as long as it does not upset the cat's digestion.

After about two or three weeks, some mother cats like to move their kittens to a new nest site, carefully lifting each one by the back of its neck and moving it to the appointed place. Usually, if the original bed or box is moved to the new site as well, the cat will accept this arrangement quite happily. Of course, the new place may not be so convenient as the old from the owner's point of view.

Newborn kittens usually suckle at two-hourly intervals and weigh between 90 to 140 grams at birth. They grow very rapidly and are consequently soon able to take in more food, and the time between feeds stretches to three to four hours. Coinciding with this, the kittens' eyes open at about eleven or twelve days old and their mother is now leaving them for short periods of time. The kittens begin to explore their surroundings, becoming more physically competent as their level of activity increases. By about three weeks of age, they will be finding their way out of the box and following their mother to the food bowl and litter tray. At this stage the mother cat will probably be encouraging her family to use the litter tray and starting the process of toilet training (*see* TRAINING—Toilet Training, page 56). The kittens should be treated for roundworms at about this age, and this needs to be repeated at regular intervals. A veterinary surgeon should be consulted about a worming programme for both the kittens and the mother cat. (*See also* PARASITES—Internal Parasites, page 128, and GROOMING AND CARE—Worming, page 70.) From now on, the kittens enjoy playing and exploring and may end up in unfamiliar corners. The mother cat calls to them to come to her if she feels that they are straying too far away or may carry them back if necessary. As they get older, the queen may find it necessary to discipline them from time to time, using growls or a bat with a front paw.

Weaning

When the kittens are three to four weeks of age, the queen will probably show signs of growing tired of continually feeding them. She limits the times that she allows suckling and may get up and walk away once she has had enough. At this stage they can be encouraged to lap cows' milk or a proprietary cat milk substitute, starting with small quantities about three or four times each day. After one or two days a little baby cereal can be added to the milk, and once this is accepted, finely minced and cooked chicken, meat or fish can be offered in small amounts. A flat dish makes feeding easier for the kittens, and their natural curiosity usually encourages them to show interest in the food. Some strategies can be employed to help the process along, such as introducing a small taste of the food into the kitten's mouth from the back of a plastic teaspoon. Once they have got used to the idea, kittens are normally eager to eat solid food, and by about five weeks of age, they can be given about four teaspoonfuls four times a day. They should also be given additional drinks of milk so that by six to eight weeks they no longer need to be fed by their mother. At this stage, the queen will probably have got tired of her family and may have ceased to permit suckling. This coincides with the time, generally three or four weeks after weaning, when the queen comes into season again and starts calling. The timing of this is variable and depends upon when the kittens were weaned and/or taken away to new homes. If the queen is not to be permitted to have any more kittens, then a veterinary surgeon should be consulted as to the best time to have her spayed.

Rearing Orphan Kittens

Because of the constant care and commitment that are required, especially during the first two weeks, it is extremely difficult to try to rear kittens that have been orphaned at birth. If there are just one or two kittens, or if the feeding is going to be for only a short time (for example, if the mother cat has had a Caesarean section), it may be worthwhile to try to feed the kittens artificially, although one should not underestimate the difficulties involved. It must be pointed out that some experts think it unwise to make the attempt, believing that without their mother a kitten cannot learn how to become a cat. They believe that orphaned kittens are destined to become unsociable adults with behavioural problems. Others, however, hold the opposite view and have successfully reared kittens that have become affectionate adult cats. It is always best to try to find a substitute mother. A nursing cat may be persuaded to accept one or two extra kittens if they are placed among her own litter during her absence. It is worth telephoning the veterinary clinic or an animal welfare centre to see if they can help.

If the decision is taken to attempt to rear the kittens, they need to be kept in a very warm place at a temperature of about 28°C during the first two weeks of life. The temperature can be lowered over the succeeding weeks although the kittens must still be kept in warm surroundings of about 21°C. A well-covered hot-water bottle should be kept in the box to provide warmth and comfort. The kittens need to be fed every two hours during their first fortnight of life with a proprietary cat milk substitute that can be obtained from a veterinary clinic. Suitable feeding bottles can also be obtained from pet stores, or a plastic syringe or eye dropper can be used. These must be sterilized before use, and it is easiest to use a solution designed for use with baby feeding utensils. Each kitten needs about 5 millilitres of milk at first, with the quantity gradually increasing according to need. The milk formula should be carefully made up according to the instructions, and it should be given at blood heat (38°C). It may be difficult to persuade a kitten to feed at first, and great care must be taken to ensure that none of the milk is inhaled. After each feed, the kitten must have its face washed using warm water and a piece of cotton wool. Clean water and a fresh pad of cotton wool should be used to wipe the abdomen and anal and urogenital openings as a substitute for the licking of the mother cat. A warm clean towel should be used to dry each kitten. After two weeks, the kittens can be fed at four-hourly intervals until they are a month old. Weaning can begin early, at three to four weeks, but milk feeds are still necessary about every six hours.

Hand-reared kittens, especially if they have missed out on receiving colostrum, are more vulnerable to infection and also to digestive disorders. If a kitten shows any signs of diarrhoea (*see* A-Z OF ILLNESSES, page 173) veterinary advice and attention should be sought as a matter of urgency as this can rapidly become life-threatening. Of course, this is the case for all kittens and not just those that have been reared by hand.

Determining the Sex of Kittens

Identifying the sex of each kitten in a litter can be a problem as the urogenital openings are in similar positions. It is easier if both sexes are represented so that one can be compared with another. It is generally thought to be easier to sex kittens shortly after birth or, alternatively, when they are four weeks old. In long-coated varieties, growth of hair may soon obscure the openings so it is probably best to carry out the identification early on.

The kitten should be held in the palm of the hand or placed on a table and its tail raised. In both sexes, the upper round opening is the anus, looking like a small dot. In a female, the urogenital opening or vulva is beneath and close to the anus. It appears like an elongated vertical slit, a little broader in the centre than at the top or bottom. In the male, the urogenital opening is slightly lower down and appears as another small round dot. It may be possible to see two small swellings between the anus and the urogenital opening which are the testicles.

CARE OF AN ELDERLY CAT

Points to Look Out For

On the whole, the pet family cat of today enjoys a better quality of life than at any time in the past. Because of advances in veterinary care, good nutrition and freedom from the stresses of reproduction, many pet cats pass into a contented old age and may live to be sixteen or seventeen. However, an elderly cat does require a little more in the way of care than a younger one since some diseases and conditions are more likely to arise in old age. An old cat naturally becomes less active and adventurous and will tend to spend a great deal of time sleeping in a warm and comfortable place. Warmth is much more important for an old cat, and it should always be able to get in out of the cold and wet. An old cat is often more susceptible to infections as its immune system probably becomes less efficient at this stage. It is advisable, therefore, to keep vaccination well up-to-date and to seek early veterinary advice if your cat shows any signs of ill health (*see* GROOMING AND CARE—Vaccination, page 72). In the same way, worming is very important as an elderly cat may have less resistance to internal parasites and become debilitated as a result of their presence (*see also* GROOMING AND

CARE—Worming, page 70, and PARASITES—Internal Parasites, page 128).

An old cat requires less feeding once its activity declines but at the same time it may become a fussy eater and refuse food that was previously enjoyed. There is no harm in coaxing the cat and indulging it a little at this stage in its life by offering more tasty, highly flavoured foods from time to time. One should first check, however, that there is nothing wrong with the cat's teeth as dental problems are quite common in old age. Sometimes it is necessary for teeth to be removed under a general anaesthetic, but a cat can manage to eat very well as long as its gums are firm and healthy (*see* periodontal disease in A-Z OF ILLNESSES, page 206). Canned commercial foods are obviously useful for a cat that has dental problems as they are soft. Constipation, which can be so severe that the animal fails to pass any motions at all, can be a problem in an elderly cat. This is sometimes caused by a loss of normal muscle tone in the bowel, and veterinary attention is needed to improve the situation (*see also* A-Z OF ILLNESSES, page 166).

Cancerous tumours (*see* A-Z OF ILLNESSES, page 222) are more common in older cats, and symptoms and treatment depend upon the site and nature of the malignancy. Regrettably, treatment by means of surgery, drugs (chemotherapy) or radiation (radiotherapy) may not effect a cure but much can usually be done to alleviate symptoms, at least for a while. Heart disease and kidney failure (*see* A-Z OF ILLNESSES, pages 194, 199) are two other disorders that are more likely to arise in elderly cats, and, depending upon severity, drug treatments can often relieve the symptoms for a time and improve the quality of life. With all these conditions, however, the time may come when the kindest course of action is to have the cat put painlessly to sleep.

Arthritis is more common in older cats, often noticed as stiffness, particularly on first getting up after resting. An old cat may not keep its claws in good order, and it may be necessary to have these trimmed from time to time (*see also* A-Z OF ILLNESSES, page 156).

PARASITES

The parasites that affect cats can be divided into two types. Internal parasites live inside the cat, mainly within the digestive tract, while external ones inhabit the fur and skin.

Internal Parasites

The internal parasites that commonly affect cats are worms belonging to two main groups, *roundworms*, or ascarids, and *tapeworms*. These develop into mature worms inside the digestive system of the cat where they live by absorbing partially digested food. Each has a different and quite complex life cycle that may involve another host animal, and an understanding of this is important in the control of worm infestation. All cats contract worms at some stage but usually, unless the infestation is very severe, they cause little harm and can be effectively dealt with by using modern drugs. These are often in the form of tablets but may be as a liquid or syrup that can be mixed with the cat's food. Worms can be a problem in a cat that is in poor health for some other reason, and, as has already been noted, young kittens are at particular risk from roundworm infestation.

128

Roundworms

Roundworms are a white or greyish colour and usually about 5 to 15 centimetres in length. They often appear to be looped or coiled and may change to a pinkish colour if they have recently absorbed food. Several worms may occur together as a tangled mass. The most common species to inhabit cats is called *Toxocara cati*. An adult worm inhabits the intestine of the cat and, occasionally, a whole parasite may be vomited up or passed out in faeces. The mature worm produces numerous minute eggs that are too small to be seen by the naked eye, and these are passed out with faeces. The eggs have a sticky surface and may adhere to the fur of the cat and be licked up and swallowed during grooming. People can get the eggs onto their fingers when handling and petting the cat. Eggs can persist for a very long time on infected ground and are extremely resistant to decay and pose a potential health risk to very young children. Each egg contains a larva that has the potential to develop into an adult worm but can do this only if it is swallowed by a cat. If ingested by other mammals, such as mice, larvae hatch from the eggs and are carried around the body in the bloodstream. They lodge in various tissues and organs and form a dormant cyst. If eggs are swallowed by a cat, the same migration of larvae, via the bloodstream, occurs through tissues and organs, including the heart, muscles, liver and lungs. Larvae in the lungs may be coughed up into the mouth and swallowed once again. In adult female cats, some larvae become lodged in the tissues and remain as cysts, causing no further harm. Other larvae return to the intestine and develop into adult worms producing more eggs, but these are safely and effectively eliminated by worming with a suitable drug (*see* GROOMING AND CARE, page 70). A veterinary surgeon can advise on the type of preparation and frequency of use. A cat may be infected directly by swallowing eggs or, quite commonly, by eating encysted larvae present in the tissues of prey animals such as mice and rabbits. Roundworms do not usually cause any problems in adult cats.

Particular circumstances apply to a pregnant queen cat and to young kittens, and worming is vital at this time to reduce the level of infestation. During pregnancy, encysted larvae present in the tissues of the female cat become active and enter the mammary glands. They are passed to the suckling kittens in their mother's milk so that two or three weeks after birth there can be a severe infestation. Kittens with a severe infestation of roundworms can become quite ill. Symptoms include a potbellied appearance, failure to thrive, diarrhoea (*see* A-Z OF ILLNESSES, page 173) and a dull coat. Larvae in the lungs may cause coughing and noisy breathing. The only way to deal with roundworms is by repeated regular worming of both the queen and her kittens, before and after birth. A veterinary surgeon can advise on the most suitable preparation to use and on frequency of worming.

It is necessary to be vigilant about the elimination of round-worms, not only for the sake of the cat but also because of a potential danger to human health. Those most at risk are very young children who may pick up the eggs on their fingers while playing on contaminated ground and transfer them to their mouths. Any ground that has been used by cats should be regarded as suspect since eggs persist long after faeces have decayed. It is evident that kittens are likely to be infected with roundworms, and if young children have access to them then great care must be taken over hygiene. It is especially impor-tant to make sure that children wash their hands thoroughly and scrub beneath their fingernails after handling kittens. *Toxocara cati* can complete its life cycle only in cats. How-ever, if eggs are swallowed by a child (or other mammal), the larvae hatch and travel in the bloodstream, lodging and encyst-ing in various organs of the body. This condition, called vis-ceral larval migrans, can cause considerable damage to, for ex-ample, the lungs, liver and retina of the eye where abnormal granulation tissue, called granuloma, may be produced. Symp-toms include muscular pain, fever, skin rash, respiratory prob-lems, vomiting and convulsions, depending upon the organs affected. Infection can be treated with various drug prepara-tions, e.g. diethylcarbamazine and thiabendazole, but tissue damage may be permanent. It is believed that young children may be at greater risk as their immune system is immature, whereas older children and adults are more resistant to infection. Visceral larval migrans is a serious condition but fortunately it is rare. Also, it is mainly the dog roundworm that has been implicated as the cause, although the involvement of *Toxocara cati* cannot be ruled out. It is further believed that many young children with access to pets may be infected without showing any signs of ill health. If sensible precautions are followed, there should be little or no risk.

Another species of roundworm, *Toxocaris leonina*, occurs more rarely in cats and is usually picked up from prey species. *Toxocaris leonina* does not form cysts in the tissues of a cat and is not implicated in human visceral larval migrans.

Tapeworms

Tapeworms are long, thin, flat worms that are usually a white colour and resemble lengths of tape. The adult worm consists of a head, or scolex, which bears tiny hooks and suckers that attach it to the intestine of a cat. Behind the head there are a series of segments, called proglottids, which each contain male and female reproductive organs. The segments are continually produced from behind the head and mature as they pass backwards. Those at the end farthest away from the head are fully mature and contain numerous fertilized eggs. These are shed in the faeces of the cat and also pass out at other times. They usually resemble grains of white rice that may be seen to move and contract for a time. They may stick to the fur of the cat or be shed within the home, and, when dry, the outer case splits to shed the microscopic eggs. Tapeworms require an intermediate or secondary host in order to complete their life cycle and do not pass directly from one cat (the primary host) to another.

In the case of the most common tapeworm of the cat, called *Dipylidium caninum*, which also affects dogs, the intermediate host is a flea or louse. Other tapeworms, mainly *Taenia* species, have rabbits, rodents, birds, etc, as intermediate hosts. In one that occasionally affects cats, *Taenia taeniformis*, the intermediate host is a rat or mouse. If the intermediate host is a mammal, minute larvae or embryos hatch from the ingested eggs and pass through the wall of the digestive tract and enter the blood circulation. They are carried around the body and encyst in muscles and tissues. If this tissue is subsequently eaten by a cat, the larva becomes active and matures to an adult tapeworm within the intestine. It is not unusual for a cat to harbour several adult tapeworms. Commonly, cats that hunt and kill rodents and eat the carcases, are infected in this way. In the case of fleas (or lice), the minute eggs of the tapeworm are probably consumed during the larval stage when the immature insects are feeding on organic debris on the cat or within its environment. The flea, containing the cysts of the tapeworm, is swallowed by the cat while it licks and grooms itself, and the worm develops in the manner described. It is uncommon for tapeworms to cause symptoms of ill health or digestive upset in cats unless present in excessive numbers. The presence of tapeworms is usually suspected when the segments are noticed, although occasionally a cat may vomit up a whole worm. A number of preparations are available that are specifically designed to eliminate tapeworms, and a veterinary surgeon can advise on which one to use. A cat that hunts habitually should be regularly treated for tapeworms. It can also be seen that it is necessary to deal with fleas, which are very common external parasites of cats, in order to control tapeworms.

People are not usually at any risk from the common tapeworm of cats. *Echinococcus multilocularis*, a small tapeworm rarely found in some cats in parts of Europe, USA and Asia, has been known to affect human beings. In this case, a person is the intermediate host, and the larva induces an abnormal growth in the liver that can produce adverse symptoms.

Other Internal Parasites

A number of other worm parasites can affect cats, but fortunately these tend to be fairly uncommon.

Two types of hookworm can occur in cats and both feed on blood. *Uncinaria stenocephali* is uncommon in pet cats in Britain but is encountered from time to time. If present in large numbers, these parasites may cause loss of appetite and weight and failure to thrive, anaemia and diarrhoea with bleeding (*see*

A-Z OF ILLNESSES, pages 151 and 173). The worms are less than one centimetre long but can cause considerable ill health. Ancyclostoma hookworms are not found in the UK but occur in parts of the USA and Australia. They may be ingested as eggs but are also capable of burrowing through the skin, travelling in the blood circulation to the intestine. Each then develops into an adult. If present in large numbers, they can cause serious debility and anaemia.

Lungworm, *Aelurostrongylus abstrusus*, is an uncommon parasite that inhabits the air spaces of the lungs. The adult worms resemble lengths of dark thread and lay their eggs in the lungs, which develop into larvae. The larvae are coughed up into the mouth and then swallowed, passing through the digestive tract to be eliminated in the faeces. These larvae then burrow into the flesh of a slug or snail, which in its turn is eaten by a mouse or rat. If the rodent is killed and eaten by a cat, the lungworm is able to complete its life cycle and develop into an adult worm in the lungs. A severe infestation causes breathing difficulties, wasting and coughing and can make the cat quite ill.

Another worm, *Capillaria aerophila*, lives in the windpipe, or tracheae, but does not penetrate as far as the lungs. It causes coughing and breathing difficulties. Larvae are coughed up and swallowed and pass through the digestive tract to be eliminated in faeces. The cycle begins again if the larvae are swallowed by another cat.

Some other internal parasites affect cats in different parts of the world but not in Europe or the United Kingdom. These are mentioned in the A-Z OF ILLNESSES, INJURIES AND VETERINARY PROCEDURES, which begins on page 149.

External Parasites

External parasites live on the skin and among the fur of cats where they make a living either by biting and sucking blood or by feeding on the flakes of debris. Various types can occur, including fleas, mites, lice and ticks.

Fleas

Most cats are probably affected by fleas at some stage in their life, and recent surveys have shown that these parasites are indeed very common. The most common type in the UK is the *Ctenophalides felis*, affecting both cats and dogs. The dog flea, *Ctenophalides canis*, is relatively rare. Occasionally a cat may pick up different species of fleas from other animals—hedgehogs, birds, rabbits or even humans—but the usual source is other cats. Fleas do not complete their life cycle on the cat, but females must obtain a meal of blood before they can lay their eggs. Adult fleas are present on the cat only for the purpose of feeding so that they can mate and reproduce. For every flea actually found on the cat, there are many others, in the form of eggs, larvae or pupae, in the animal's environment. Fleas can easily be seen when present, if the hair of the cat is parted, as small, brown insects moving around rapidly. Favourite places for them to congregate are the base of the ears and tail. Often, rather than the insects themselves being detected, the faeces of the fleas, which consist of remnants of dried blood, are noticed caught in the fur as small black specks resembling grit. If these are sponged with a moist paper towel or cotton wool, a red-brown stain appears so it is easy to differentiate between flea faeces and other dirt.

Having obtained a meal of blood, a female flea usually drops off the cat to lay her eggs in the immediate environment. Common sites are the cat's bed and bedding but also chairs, beds, carpets and even the spaces between floorboards. Eggs are smooth and non-sticky and if laid directly on the cat soon drop off to be deposited elsewhere. They hatch into larvae that feed on minute particles of organic debris, including the flea dirts of adult insects, and they may ingest tapeworm eggs at this stage. The larvae pupate, and adult fleas emerge in favourable conditions when it is warm and humid. In general, adult fleas begin to emerge and breed in the spring and summer months, their numbers peaking in August and September. Flea pupae can exist for many months in this state until environmental conditions are favourable for hatching. In optimum conditions, however, which include modern, centrally heated homes, the whole life cycle from egg to breeding adult flea takes only two to three weeks. A female flea may produce as many as 500 eggs in her lifetime.

It is evident that in order to control fleas both the cat and its surroundings must be treated. Many insecticidal preparations are available for eliminating fleas, some of which are used on the animal itself and others for treating the home environment. A veterinary surgeon is the best person to consult about which of these to use. Preventative measures to protect the cat from acquiring fleas include insecticidal tablets that are fed to the animal, solutions applied to the skin and flea collars. Various sprays, powders and shampoos can be used to kill any fleas that are present and to afford some protection against further colonization. Since cats are so constant and thorough in grooming, great care must be exercised with anything applied to the coat. It is all too easy for a cat to ingest a toxic dose of insecticide, and this is why veterinary advice is so important. Instructions on product containers should be strictly followed. Some modern flea treatments are designed to be used as an attack on two fronts, i.e. on the cat and its home surroundings, and these are usually very effective. It is important to remember that all the cats and dogs in a home must be treated at the same time and not just the one that is suspected of harbouring fleas. Regular washing of the cat's bed and bedding helps to control fleas, as does thorough vacuuming of all carpets, chairs and soft furnishings.

Fleas may harbour the immature stage of the tapeworm, *Dipylidium caninum*, and it may be necessary subsequently to worm a cat that has been affected. Fleas can also transmit infectious diseases from one cat to another, and a severe infestation of these parasites can even result in anaemia, especially in young kittens. Even a few bites are highly irritating and may cause the cat to scratch and bite itself, thereby damaging the skin, with the possibility of secondary bacterial infection. Some cats also suffer from a hypersensitive allergic reaction to even a few flea bites. The skin becomes irritated and inflamed and 'weeps', and this is usually noticed on the animal's back, especially towards the base of its tail. This condition is known as miliary eczema, and scabby crusts form on the skin that are very itchy (*see* A-Z OF ILLNESSES, page 175). The animal requires veterinary treatment to clear up the condition, as well as elimination of the fleas.

Mites

There are several types of mite that can affect cats, but only one, the ear mite, can be regarded as common. Some species of mite are visible to the human eye whereas others can be seen only with the aid of a microscope. Mites are not insects but belong to the class Arachnida, which includes spiders, scorpions and ticks. Mites and ticks are the parasitic members of the group whereas most are free-living.

Ear Mites

After fleas, the ear mite *Otodectes cyanotis* is the most common and troublesome external parasite to affect both cats and dogs. The mites are barely visible to the human eye and inhabit the inner surface of the external ear canal, where they can sometimes be seen as minute grey specks moving over the surface. They do not pierce the skin but live on debris composed mainly of dead shed skin, wax and lymph fluid that leaks out as a result of the cat's excessive scratching.

The symptoms of ear mites are continual scratching, rubbing and shaking of the ears, and the cat's head may be held on one side. The presence of the mites is so irritating that the cat claws at its ears, causing bleeding and bare patches on the outside where the fur is rubbed off.

The inside of the ear flap may become wet and sticky, and there is a buildup of hard, brown wax, which, when examined under a microscope, betrays the presence of the mites. A cat with any sign of ear irritation should be taken to a veterinary surgeon for diagnosis and treatment. The veterinary surgeon will examine the ear with the aid of an auroscope or otoscope and may obtain a sample of wax. Delay is likely to lead to a worsening of the situation, and there may be a secondary bacterial infection as a result of the scratching.

Treatment is by means of ear drops that contain chemicals designed to kill the mites. Some preparations combine these with antibacterial drugs, agents for softening ear wax and local anaesthetics. These combinations help to relieve the pain and irritation and deal with any secondary bacterial infection that may have gained access through the broken skin. Usually it is necessary to continue the treatment for some time to make sure that all newly emerging mites are killed. In addition, both ears should be treated at the same time, even if the symptoms appear to be confined to one, and all dogs and cats in the household must be given simultaneous treatment as the mites are very contagious.

Ear mites are so intensely irritating that the cat will react very strongly to both the examination of its ears and the treatment. In some cases it may be necessary to sedate the animal or even to give a general anaesthetic. In order to carry out treatment at home, it is wise to wear gloves and to wrap up the cat firmly in an old blanket or towel, leaving its head free but making sure that the limbs are immobilized.

Mange Mites

Mange is an uncommon condition in cats, but, when it does occur, one of two types of mite may be responsible.

The minute, microscopic mange mite *Notoedres cati* is responsible for the feline form of scabies or notoedric mange. This is a very contagious skin disease that readily spreads from one cat to another. The mites live and breed in burrows within the upper layers of skin and cause very severe irritation. The infestation usually begins at the ear tips and spreads downwards across the forehead and the rest of the face. The cat tries to relieve the irritation by rubbing its head against objects and using its paws, and the mites may then be transferred to these as well. The hair is rubbed off and falls out and the skin becomes thickened, wrinkled and scabby.

Demodectic or follicular mange (demodecosis) is rarer still in cats and is caused by another type of microscopic mite, *Demodex canis*, which is a common parasite of dogs. The mites inhabit the hair follicles, and in cats the infestation usually affects the skin surrounding the eyes and the eyelids. Bare, reddened patches appear as the hairs fall out and there may be a musty smell.

Diagnosis of both forms of mite infestation is normally carried out at a veterinary clinic by microscopic examination of skin samples. Treatment is by means of the various insecticidal preparations that are used to control fleas and are also effective against mites. These parasites cannot survive for long away from their host animal so extensive repeated treatment of the cat's environment is not necessary. Since notoedric mange is so contagious, however, the affected animal should be isolated from others, but all cats in contact must be treated at the same time. The bed and bedding of the cat or cats should be boil-washed or disinfected.

Cheyletiella (Fur) Mites

Fur mites, *Cheyletiella blakei*, are very small, but it is just possible to see them with the naked eye. They are an uncommon parasite of cats and can be present without causing any irritation at all, although in some animals there is severe itching and consequent scratching. The most characteristic sign of infestation is the appearance of prolific scurf or dandruff, especially along the back of the cat, with a greasy feel to the fur. This consists of the mites and their eggs, and if it is examined closely, it can be seen to be moving. The name 'walking dandruff' is an apt description of this infestation by parasites that spend their entire life upon the cat. A cat with these symptoms should be examined by a veterinary surgeon, and treatment is similar to that given for mange mites (*see* page 141) and fleas (*see* page 136). The mites are either acquired directly from other cats or via grooming equipment or bedding. Hence all cats in the home must be treated at the same time, and it is wise to boil-wash or disinfect beds and bedding. People handling the cat should exercise caution, and it is wise to wear gloves and to wash hands thoroughly. The mite may cause irritation in people with sensitive skins, and young children are likely to be particularly susceptible. Small, itchy, reddened patches appear on the skin, especially on the arms as these are in contact when a person lifts the cat. These turn yellowish and scabby as a result of scratching.

Harvest Mites

Harvest mites can affect country-dwelling cats in particular in the later months of the summer or early autumn. It is the larvae of these mites that are parasitic, and cats normally pick them up as they pass through long grass or other dense vegetation. The larvae attach themselves to areas where the skin is less tough, such as on the ears, paws and lower legs, where they feed and grow. Eventually they drop off and develop into adult mites that feed on rotting vegetation. Harvest mite larvae can be detected as tiny reddish-coloured specks that cause inflammation, irritation and scratching. They are treated with similar preparations that are used against other types of mite.

Lice

Lice are tiny, wingless insects that spend their whole life on their host animal. They are rare parasites of pet cats, although they are more common on farm-dwelling and stray animals. The cat louse, *Felicola subrostratus*, is a flat, flesh-coloured insect that feeds on flakes of dead skin and other debris within the fur. It is a biting louse, and an infestation may cause few symptoms or there may be severe skin irritation and scratching. A severe infestation is more likely to cause problems such as anaemia and loss of condition in elderly or ill cats and young kittens. The infestation may be noticed because of the apparent presence of dandruff or scurf. This consists of the eggs and egg cases (nits) of the lice, each of which is firmly stuck to a hair. These can be removed by using a fine-toothed comb or by cutting off the affected hairs. If it is suspected that a cat has lice, diagnosis should be confirmed by a veterinary surgeon. A specific regime may need to be followed to eradicate these parasites, using insecticidal shampoos or other preparations. The treatment normally needs to be repeated because it kills only the adult insects and not the eggs, and must be continued until all newly emerged lice are eliminated.

Ticks

Like mites, ticks are parasitic members of the class Arachnida, which includes spiders, and are not insects. They are uncommon parasites of cats, and the most likely one to be encountered is the species found on hedgehogs, *Ixodes hexagonus*. Other species found in moorland and upland areas are normally parasitic on sheep but can also affect cats living in country areas. Cats usually acquire ticks during the warm summer months after going through thick grass and other dense vegetation. A tick has piercing, biting mouth parts and fastens itself firmly onto the skin, often on the inside of the thighs or abdomen, ears, head or neck. A tick is quite small when it first latches on to the cat but is still easily visible as a small, dark-coloured protuberance with short, black, waving legs. It may be quite difficult to detect amongst a cat's dense fur. The tick feeds on blood and swells to become quite large, often turning a pinkish-orange colour. A cat may not seem to be bothered by its presence, but it can also be intensely painful and irritating.

An attempt can be made to remove the tick, but it is important to do this correctly and to make sure that all the parasite is removed. A common mistake is to try to pull off the tick, but this merely separates the abdomen from the rest of the body and leaves the head and mouth parts firmly embedded in the skin. When this happens, there is a risk of the development of a painful and septic skin abscess (*see* A-Z OF ILLNESSES, page 150). The correct method is to 'anaesthetize' the parasite by applying a pad of cotton wool soaked in surgical spirit, alcohol or insecticidal solution to induce the mouth parts to relax. The body of the tick should then be grasped with tweezers or fingers and moved from side to side and then twisted in an anticlockwise direction, when it is to be hoped the whole body will be dislodged. If this fails, a veterinary surgeon can supply a suitable preparation that will kill the tick and provide some protection against further infestation.

If it is not detected, a tick eventually drops off its host when sufficiently engorged with blood in order to breed and complete its life cycle. Ticks can attach themselves to any suitable passing mammal, including cats, dogs and people.

There has been increasing concern recently about a bacterial infection transmitted by ticks called Lyme disease. The bacteria are passed on by the bite of an infected tick and cause a potentially serious inflammatory illness in people, early signs of which are a characteristic red skin rash and 'flu-like symptoms. Not all ticks carry these bacteria, but it is important to take these parasites seriously and to destroy, by burning, any that are removed from a cat. People who walk in an area where ticks are known to be present are advised to wear long trousers tucked into boots, to avoid dense vegetation and to report to their doctor if they become ill after receiving a tick bite.

Flies and Bluebottles

Common blowflies or bluebottles are attracted to rotting organic matter and also to wounds and sores on a living animal. If a wound on a cat is left untreated or is not noticed, and the animal is weak and ill, these flies may lay their eggs in the sore. These soon hatch into larvae or maggots that feed on the flesh, and this situation is commonly called 'fly strike'. It may occasionally be a problem in an elderly or debilitated cat or one that is a stray. The animal should be taken to a veterinary surgeon so that the wound can be cleansed and treated, and the cat is likely to need antibiotics and other medication, depending upon its condition. If left untreated, this condition is potentially very serious as some cats may pass into shock (*see* A-Z OF ILLNESSES, page 217) as a result of toxins produced by the maggots passing into the bloodstream.

In other countries of the world, cats are affected by different external and internal parasites, some of which can transmit unpleasant illnesses. Some of these are described in the following section.

In the UK, cats can be affected by the ringworm fungus that produces similar skin lesions to those of external parasites and is also highly contagious to man. Ringworm is described in more detail on page 215 in the next section.

A-Z OF ILLNESSES, INJURIES AND VETERINARY PROCEDURES

In this section cross-references to other topics within the section are indicated by lowercase small capitals.

abdominal pain pain in the abdomen can arise from a number of different causes, varying from mild to severe, and treatment is governed by this. The pain may be a symptom of an illness, digestive upset, blockage in the intestine, such as a FUR BALL, or the cat may have swallowed a FOREIGN BODY. The cat may show obvious signs of discomfort or pain, e.g. resenting being handled or crying out if an attempt is made to lift it up. It may be apathetic and uninterested in what is happening, lie down or sleep more than is usual, refuse food and fail to carry out normal activities such as grooming. A well-wrapped, warm hot-water bottle may provide some relief and comfort, but the cat should be taken immediately to the veterinary surgery for examination and diagnosis. X-rays may need to be taken and, possibly, surgery to correct the problem. The cat should therefore not be given food or drink in case a general ANAESTHETIC is needed.

abscess cats are particularly susceptible to the formation of abscesses, especially as a result of BITES or scratches received in fights. An abscess is a collection of pus at a localized site anywhere in the body. It usually appears as a painful, hot swelling beneath the skin, which enlarges, comes to a head and bursts when ripe. The release of pus, and usually some blood, from the abscess brings relief from pain. In addition to having a painful lump, the cat may seem off-colour, refusing food and running a temperature. The animal should be seen by a veterinary surgeon who will usually prescribe a course of antibiotics to kill off the bacteria causing the infection. It may be necessary for the cat to have the abscess lanced and surgically drained under a general ANAESTHETIC so do not give anything to eat or drink. In some cases, the veterinary surgeon may advise bathing the swelling with hot water containing salts such as Epsom Salts or antiseptic solution and applying hot dressings (fomentations) until it bursts. Further bathing several times a day is then needed, and the wound must be kept open until all the pus has drained out. It may be necessary to pack the wound with sterile gauze to prevent it from closing too soon or else a fresh abscess may develop near the site.

allergic reactions cats may occasionally suffer from allergic skin reactions as a result of flea bites (*see* PARASITES—External Parasites, page 136), the wearing of flea collars or in response to an insect BITE or STING or an injection. The affected site may become swollen, itchy and painful or the face may swell. Veterinary advice and attention is needed, and applying a cold compress may be helpful to reduce the swelling. An allergic reaction can sometimes be a prelude to the serious but rare condition of ANAPHYLACTIC SHOCK.

alopecia *see* BALDNESS.

anaemia a decrease in the ability of the blood to carry oxygen because of a reduction in the number of red blood cells or in the amount of haemoglobin that they contain. Haemoglobin is the iron-containing pigment in red blood cells that binds to oxygen. Anaemia is a symptom of some underlying disorder or illness, and three main types are recognized in cats. The first type is the result of actual loss of blood or haemorrhage from ruptured blood vessels (haemorrhagic anaemia). This is obvious in the case of an external wound, but BLEEDING producing anaemia can occur internally following injury. A great infestation with external or internal blood-sucking parasites (*see also* PARASITES, page 128) can be responsible, as can ingestion of certain poisons (*see* POISONING). An example of such a poison is warfarin, which is sometimes used to kill rats and causes haemorrhage and prevention of blood clotting.

A second type of anaemia results from some form of damage or deficiency in the bone marrow, which is responsible for the production of red blood cells (hypoplastic anaemia). In cats, the most usual cause is ingestion of certain drugs, i.e. accidental POISONING, e.g. by insecticides. A cat's liver is ill equipped to neutralize toxic substances, and damage to the bone marrow may be the result. A much rarer cause of hypoplastic anaemia is a bone marrow tumour or a dietary deficiency. Aspirin is especially harmful to cats, causing internal haemorrhages (a condition known as haemorrhagic anaemia) and long-lasting bone marrow effects (hypoplastic anaemia) and liver damage. Thirdly, haemolytic anaemia occurs if for some reason the red blood cells that are being produced normally are destroyed and removed from the circulation. Toxic substances released by bacteria and ingestion of some chemical poisons can be responsible and also the illnesses FELINE INFECTIOUS ANAEMIA and FELINE LEUKAEMIA.

Symptoms of anaemia include extreme pallor of the lips, gums and tongue (and also the inner eyelids). In many cats, however, these mucous membranes normally appear pale so this can be difficult to interpret. Further signs include tiredness, lack of energy, rapid breathing and (in extreme cases) raised heartbeat rate even without exertion. A cat showing any signs of anaemia should be seen by a veterinary surgeon so that the underlying cause can be established and treated.

anaesthesia and **anaesthetic** anaesthesia is a loss of sensation or feeling in the whole or part of the body, usually as a result of the administration of anaesthetic drugs so that surgery can be performed. A general anaesthetic produces a loss of sensation in the whole of the body and a 'local' in only one part. General anaesthetics also cause a loss of consciousness, and often combinations of drugs are used to achieve an optimum effect, i.e. to deaden pain and relax muscles, enabling surgical procedures to be carried out with no awareness on the part of the patient. Local anaesthetic blocks the transmission of nerve impulses in the area where they are applied so that little or no pain is felt.

The great majority of surgical procedures carried out on cats are performed under general anaesthesia. This removes the fear and trauma that the cat might suffer if it remained conscious and ensures that the animal remains perfectly still. In some cases it may be necessary to administer a general anaesthetic even to examine and investigate a painful disorder, particularly if the cat is aggressive and/or very frightened. As with human patients, a cat should not be given anything to eat or drink for a number of hours before it receives a general anaesthetic to ensure that it has an empty stomach. This reduces the risk of VOMITING and inhalation of material into the lungs, causing PNEUMONIA. Modern drugs used to induce general anaesthesia are normally very safe, and the slight risks attached to their use are greatly outweighed by the benefits of being able to operate to correct painful injuries and disorders in cats and other animals. Veterinary surgeons are highly skilled and trained in

153

the correct use of these drugs. However, all general anaesthesia produces an element of risk and, as with people, it is usually impossible to identify in advance a cat that may react badly to a particular drug. It is known that elderly cats, young kittens and those suffering from an existing illness or weakness are likely to be at greater risk. In all cases, a general anaesthetic will not be given unless there is no alternative and it is considered to be in the animal's best interest. Hence a cat's owners are asked to sign a form consenting to both anaesthesia and surgery, and this gives an opportunity for the details of the procedure to be explained and for any questions to be answered.

The use of local anaesthetic drugs in cats is generally restricted to the treatment of skin complaints such as the removal of small TUMOURS, etc.

anaphylactic shock this is an extreme ALLERGIC reaction that may uncommonly occur in a cat following an insect sting or bite, injection or ingestion of drugs or, extremely rarely, some type of food. The animal experiences collapse, breathing difficulties, the gums turn blue and there may be VOMITING or DIARRHOEA. The cat fails to respond and is evidently extremely ill. This is an emergency and the cat requires an injection of adrenaline, which must be administered quickly in order to save its life. (*See also* artificial respiration and cardiopulmonary resuscitation in A-Z OF FIRST AID FOR CATS.)

appetite loss a loss or lowering of appetite probably occurs in all cats from time to time and the causes are variable. Sometimes the cause may be obvious, for instance it may be apparent that the cat has a painful mouth and so is reluctant to eat. A cat that has eaten something that disagrees with it and has been sick may refuse its next meal. (If a cat has been sick, it is usually advisable to withhold food for a few hours—*see* VOMITING.) A loss of appetite in cats is often a first sign of illness and may or may not be accompanied by other early symptoms such as lethargy, raised temperature and heartbeat rate, and dull eyes and coat. KIDNEY DISEASE and respiratory illnesses, which depress the ability to smell and taste food, often cause a disinclination to eat. Also, cats that are recovering from illness or injury may refuse food, and a convalescent animal may need considerable coaxing to persuade it to eat (*see* DIET—Underfeeding, Weight Loss, Feeding a Sick Cat, page 50). As a general rule it is best to observe the cat closely and, if the problem persists, to take it to a veterinary surgeon for further investigation. There may be a simple explanation, such as the presence of a FUR BALL in the stomach that is making the animal feel full.

It should also be appreciated that cats are highly sensitive animals, and a loss of appetite can occur as a result of psychological or emotional trauma. Causes include being placed in a cattery, arrival of a new pet or baby, disturbance in the house, such as DIY activities and decorating, and changes in the normal routine. Highly strung pedigree cats, e.g. Siamese and Burmese, may be more susceptible. Usually these problems can be overcome by sympathetic handling and understanding of the cat's needs and are resolved in a short time.

Some cats hate to be watched while eating, particularly by unfamiliar people, and this is likely to be a problem with wary, nervous strays. It is also quite normal for both toms and queens to be less interested in food when overcome by the urge to mate.

arthritis inflammation of the joints, which may affect elderly cats. It is usually noticed as lameness on first rising after a period of rest or as a generalized stiffness and a loss of the graceful fluidity of movement that is so much a feature of cats. It is essential for the cat to be examined by a veterinary surgeon to rule out other possible reasons for the symptoms. There is no cure for arthritis, but various drugs are available that can relieve the symptoms, and warmth is particularly helpful.

ascites a collection of fluid in the abdomen, giving a potbellied appearance. It is usually caused by an illness, particularly FELINE INFECTIOUS PERITONITIS or by a TUMOUR.

asphyxia a state of suffocation during which breathing eventually stops and oxygen fails to reach the tissues and organs.

Cases include drowning, strangulation, e.g. from a cat collar that becomes caught, an inhaled object blocking the windpipe and breathing in poisonous fumes. Asphyxia can also occur as a result of ANAPHYLACTIC SHOCK, when the throat and respiratory passages may swell and prevent air from reaching the lungs. Asphyxia is an emergency, requiring prompt intervention in order to save the cat's life in the form of artificial respiration (*see* A-Z OF FIRST AID FOR CATS, page 226).

Aujesky's disease *see* PSEUDORABIES.

bad breath (halitosis) it is not uncommon for older cats to develop bad breath, and this is nearly always related to disorders of the teeth and gums, particularly an ABSCESS or PERIODONTAL DISEASE. Kittens that are losing their milk teeth and acquiring their permanent ones may sometimes develop bad breath. Rarely, the milk teeth fail to come out as the adult ones come through, and this can cause infection, mouth ULCERS and bad breath. In cats of any age, a piece of food or bone that has become firmly lodged in the teeth may be a cause of bad breath. A far less common reason is the presence of a growth or TUMOUR. The cause of bad breath should always be investigated and diagnosed by a veterinary surgeon so that appropriate treatment can be given. Bad breath may be a symptom of KIDNEY DISEASE (URAEMIA) in older cats.

baldness (alopecia) true loss of hair or baldness is really quite rare in cats. Usually the appearance of bald patches in the cat is the result of some form of skin disorder, often the presence of external parasites or ECZEMA. A less common cause is hypothyroidism (myxoedema), in which there is a lack of the hormones produced by the thyroid gland. Patchy hair loss in a cat should always be investigated by a veterinary surgeon so that the underlying cause can be established and appropriate treatment given. (*See also* PARASITES—External Parasites, page 136.)

bee and wasp stings cats may be at risk from stings and bites, particularly young and playful animals that chase after insects. Stings on the body are painful but unless they are numerous should not usually prove harmful. A bee sting is likely to be left in the skin and continues to discharge its poison. The complete sting should be carefully removed with tweezers, and this can be tricky since it is barbed. Stings can be bathed with cold water or a solution of half a pint of water containing one teaspoonful of sodium bicarbonate. A cold ice pack or compress can be applied to reduce any localized swelling. The danger arises if the cat is stung on its tongue as this may then swell and block the windpipe, causing breathing difficulties. A further risk is that of ANAPHYLACTIC SHOCK, which can be caused by an insect sting in a hypersensitive individual. A cat that is experiencing breathing difficulties needs immediate veterinary attention, and it may be necessary to attempt artificial respiration (*see* A-Z OF FIRST AID FOR CATS, page 226) in order to save its life. Unfortunately, however, if there is a great deal of swelling in the region of the throat this may not be successful.

biopsy an aid to diagnosis that involves removing a small sample of living tissue from the body for examination under the microscope. The technique can be used to distinguish between benign and malignant TUMOURS. This procedure is one that would normally be carried out under a general ANAESTHETIC.

bites most cats receive bites at some time or other, most commonly either during fights or from a prey animal such as a rat. Superficial bits can be bathed with an antiseptic solution, but deeper or more extensive wounds are likely to require veterinary attention and stitching. Since there is a great risk of ABSCESS formation with any bite, it is wise to seek veterinary advice as the cat may need a course of antibiotics to combat infection. Rarely, in upland and moorland countryside, a cat may be bitten by an adder. If this occurs it should be kept calm and quiet and taken for veterinary treatment immediately, as it will require an injection of antidote for adder venom. Cats are much less likely to be bitten than dogs, and so are at a lower risk from the highly venomous snakes that live in some parts of the world.

bladder stones *see* FELINE UROLOGICAL SYNDROME.

bladder worm a species of parasitic worm that affects cats in Australia.

blastomycosis a rare respiratory illness affecting cats in certain parts of the USA and caused by a fungus.

blisters small, fluid-filled sores beneath the surface of the skin that do not usually occur in cats but may arise as a result of a BURN or frictional injury. A minor blister can be bathed with warm water containing antiseptic solution, dried and covered with a clean dressing. (*See also* A-Z OF FIRST AID FOR CATS, page 232.)

blood samples and transfusions in the case of illness, it may sometimes be necessary to obtain blood samples to aid diagnosis or check on a cat's progress, and this is carried out by a veterinary surgeon. Similarly, a cat that is very ill and hospitalized, may occasionally require blood transfusions, generally as a result of serious injuries or during or after a major operation.

breathing problems breathing problems are a fairly common occurrence in cats, and the cause should always be established by a veterinary surgeon. Some of the causes are FELINE RESPIRATORY DISEASE or cat 'flu, BRONCHITIS, infestation by certain internal parasites (*see* PARASITES—Internal Parasites, page 128), malignant lung TUMOURS and HEART DISEASE. Symptoms include laboured noisy breathing, especially after exercise, coughing and panting.

burns and scalds *see* A-Z OF FIRST AID FOR CATS, page 232.

Caesarean section surgical delivery of a litter, normally carried out as an emergency procedure by a veterinary surgeon when it is apparent that labour and birth are not going to proceed successfully. This may be because of an awkward presentation so that a kitten has become stuck or ineffective contractions of the womb (uterine inertia). Speed is of the essence if a Caesarean delivery is to be successful in saving the life of a queen cat and her kittens, but it is normally very effective. The cat is anaesthetized and the kittens are delivered via an incision through the wall of the abdomen and another made directly into the womb. The wounds are sutured, and although the queen needs extra care and help following the operation, she can usually feed and care for her kittens in the normal way.

cancer a widely used term describing any form of malignant TUMOUR. Characteristically there is an abnormal growth of cancer cells which invade surrounding tissues and destroy them. Cancer cells may spread throughout the body via the bloodstream or lymphatic system, a process known as metastasis,

161

and set up secondary growths elsewhere. In common with human beings, cats are subject to a range of cancerous conditions. The most frequently occurring forms are lymphomas affecting lymph tissue of the lymph nodes, spleen and thymus gland and also the kidneys, nasal passages and nervous system. These account for about one third of all malignancies in cats and, unusually, are quite common in young animals. Most cancers are more common with increasing age and, unfortunately, cats appear to be quite susceptible. Other common sites include the mouth, skin and mammary glands in female animals, although growths can occur anywhere in the body.

Secondary growths quite commonly arise in the lungs, causing BREATHING PROBLEMS and coughing. Symptoms caused by a cancer vary according to its site within the body. If a lump is detected or symptoms of illness are noticed, the cat should be taken to a veterinary surgeon for further investigation. Possible forms of treatment include surgery, chemotherapy (drug therapy) and radiotherapy (X-ray radiation). As in human medicine, some malignancies can be successfully treated if caught early, particularly those on the skin. It may be possible to relieve symptoms at least for a time, but in some cases the kindest option is to have the cat put to sleep.

candidiasis an uncommon condition in cats, producing sores on the skin and in the mouth, caused by the yeast organism

Candida albicans, which produces thrush infections in people. The condition is treated with antifungal drugs.

canker a popular term used to describe ear problems in cats and dogs in which there is itching, a sticky discharge that may smell and a buildup of wax. In cats it is almost always caused by the presence of ear mites (*see* PARASITES—External Parasites, page 136).

car sickness *see* TRAVEL SICKNESS.

castration *see* NEUTERING.

cataract a condition in which the lens of the eye becomes opaque or clouded, resulting in a blurring or even total loss of vision. It is not common but may arise in elderly cats.

catarrh irritation and inflammation of mucous membranes (but generally taken to refer to the nasal passages and airways) with the production and discharge of a thick mucus. As in people, a discharge from the nose, often accompanied by sneezing and breathing difficulties, is an indication of some disorder, usually FELINE RESPIRATORY DISEASE or cat influenza. Often the cat's sense of smell and taste is affected, and the animal refuses food and is apathetic and ill. A cat with catarrh should be taken for veterinary examination and treatment.

cat mint (cat nip) a plant, *Nepeta cataria*, that is immensely attractive to cats, producing alterations in behaviour. The cat may roll or rub itself against the plant, or objects containing oils from it, and it is often added to toys.

choking *see* A-Z OF FIRST AID FOR CATS, page 235.

claws (broken or infected) occasionally a cat may break a claw and the core becomes exposed, causing great pain and LAMENESS. A bacterial infection can arise at the base of a claw, whether it is broken or not, leading to the development of an ABSCESS. It is usually obvious if there is something wrong with a paw or claw as, in addition to pain and lameness, the cat will continually lick the affected area. The animal should be taken to a veterinary surgeon for examination and treatment. It should not be given anything to eat or drink in case a general ANAESTHETIC and corrective surgery are needed.

claws (clipping) elderly or ill cats may be unable to keep their nails in good order, and these may grow too long and need to be trimmed. It is advisable for this to be carried out by a veterinary surgeon in the first instance, who can then show you how to trim the claws at home. It is usually advisable for two people to be involved, one to restrain the cat and the other to carry out the trimming. It is best to use special clippers designed for the purpose, which can be obtained from a veterinary surgery. The golden rule is to remember that there can be considerable BLEEDING if too much of the claw is taken off and the quick is exposed. It is far better to take off a little more frequently than a lot all at once, and this is the reason why veterinary advice is so important at first.

cleft palate a relatively common congenital birth defect in newborn kittens in which an opening is left in the midline of the palate which has failed to fuse during development. Hence there is an opening between the mouth and the nasal chambers so that when the kitten feeds the milk tends to drip from its nose. Unless the condition is very slight, in which case a surgical repair is possible, a veterinary surgeon will normally recommend that the kitten be put humanely to sleep.

coccidiosis a relatively rare disease in cats in the United Kingdom caused by parasitic infestation by a minute protozoan microorganism. The organism inhabits the bowel and is responsible for the production of DIARRHOEA (which may contain blood), loss of weight and debility and, possibly, ANAEMIA. This condition must be diagnosed and treated by a veterinary surgeon.

coma a state of deep unconsciousness from which a cat cannot be roused. It may be accompanied by noisy breathing and a strong heart action but there is no response to painful stimuli and a lack of eye reflexes. It may arise as a result of injury to the brain, high fever caused by infection, extremes of heat and cold, DIABETES, ingestion of drugs or poisons or inhalation of poisonous fumes such as carbon monoxide. A cat in a coma requires immediate emergency veterinary attention, and treatment and prognosis depends upon cause. The animal may need artificial respiration or cardiopulmonary resuscitation if its condition deteriorates. (*See also* A-Z OF FIRST AID FOR CATS, pages 226, 234.)

conjunctivitis inflammation of the mucous membrane (conjunctiva) that lines the inside of the eyelid and covers the front of the eye. The eye becomes red and sore, and there may be a sticky discharge. It can result from a scratch or abrasion, allowing access to bacteria that cause infection. Usually it is a condition that accompanies FELINE RESPIRATORY DISEASE. The cat should be examined by a veterinary surgeon and is likely to need antibiotic eye drops or ointment. Your veterinary surgeon can show you how to apply these at home. Generally, two people are needed, one to restrain the cat on a table and the other to apply the drops or ointment.

constipation a condition in which the bowels are opened too infrequently and the faeces become hard, dry and difficult to pass. True constipation is usually only a problem in elderly cats. Apparent straining may in fact be indicative of the opposite disorder, DIARRHOEA or CYSTITIS or FELINE UROLOGICAL SYNDROME.

convulsions or **fits** involuntary, rapid and alternate contractions and relaxations of muscles throwing the body and limbs into contortions, often with partial or complete unconsciousness. Usually there is an initial trembling followed by marked contractions of the muscles, generally resulting in the animal collapsing onto the ground and thrashing its limbs and biting its jaws. Sphincter muscles controlling the bladder and anus may relax, causing urine and faeces to be voided, and the cat may salivate. If the cat is on a hard surface or close to jutting-out objects, these should be covered with cushions, blankets or coats to prevent injury. It is best not to interfere with, or try to restrain, the cat in any way unless it is in a dangerous position. In this case, the cat should have a coat or blanket placed around it so that it can be pulled clear of the hazard with less risk of the person being scratched or bitten. All sources of noise, heat and light should be switched off and the curtains drawn. A fit normally lasts for less than fifteen minutes, and as the muscular activity subsides, the cat may appear dazed, frightened and not able to see properly. It should be kept calm and quiet in a cool, darkened room and reassured by the presence of its owner while veterinary assistance is summoned. Some cats, however, may react viciously in the recovery phase or else hide under furniture in extreme fear. Occasionally fits continue, and this emergency condition is known as *status epilepticus*.

Although fits are relatively uncommon in cats, it is possible for an affected animal to have several in any one day. The most common cause is ingestion of certain poisons, but others include brain injuries or inflammation of the membranes (ENCEPHALITIS and MENINGITIS), LIVER and KIDNEY DISEASES, deficiency in the B vitamin thiamine, and a low blood calcium level in a queen cat that has recently given birth (*see* ECLAMPSIA). Sometimes the cause cannot be determined and, while drugs can be given to control recurrent convulsions, these may not be necessary if the condition is mild or unlikely to recur.

coughing as with people, a cat may cough for a number of different reasons, some of which are more serious than others. If the cough is of a transitory nature, there is no need for alarm as it may have been caused by inhalation of some irritating substance such as dust or pollen. If it is persistent or accompanied by other symptoms such as BREATHING PROBLEMS, nasal discharge, runny eyes, loss of appetite, etc, the cat should be taken for veterinary diagnosis and treatment. A cough in cats may be a symptom of FELINE RESPIRATORY DISEASE (cat influenza), HEART DISEASE or infestation by certain internal parasites. (*See also* PARASITES, page 128.)

cryptococcus a rare fungal disease affecting cats in parts of the USA, producing respiratory and nervous symptoms.

cryptorchidism and **monorchidism** a condition in which both or one of the testicles of a male tom cat fail to descend into the scrotum and are retained within the abdomen. A veterinary surgeon may advise waiting to see if the testicle(s) eventually descend(s) correctly, but if not, abdominal surgery is required for removal. This is necessary for two reasons. Firstly, the animal may behave like a true tom, and secondly, there is a greatly increased risk of CANCER in the affected testicle(s).

cystitis inflammation of the bladder, normally caused by bacterial infection and more common in queens than in male cats. The symptoms of cystitis are frequent attempts to urinate but with only a few drops being passed. The urine frequently contains blood, and the process is evidently painful. There may be other signs of illness, such as lethargy and a raised temperature. The cat should be taken to a veterinary surgeon and will normally need a course of antibiotics to kill the infection.

deafness congenital, i.e. inborn, deafness in cats frequently accompanies white coat colour and is almost always present if the adult animal also has two blue eyes. A white cat with a single blue eye is usually deaf on one side. More usually, however, deafness is a condition of old age in cats and is linked to degenerative changes in the organs of the inner ear responsible for hearing. A deaf cat is obviously at increased risk from road traffic and misses out on vocal exchanges with other cats. Frequently, a cat that is congenitally deaf is very alert in its other senses and can, for example, detect and interpret vibrations in the ground and air.

dehydration a healthy cat drinks in order to make up water that has been lost from the body through urination, elimination of faeces and respiration. If a cat is unable to make up the deficit, it will soon begin to show signs of dehydration. There is a loss of skin elasticity so that if a small portion is pinched it stays folded in that position. The cat has a dry nose and mouth as fewer secretions are produced and the coat may be dull and the eyes appear sunken. The cat is lethargic and generally unwell and, since dehydration is a feature of various diseases and disorders, there may be other symptoms. VOMITING and DIARRHOEA can soon produce dehydration, but water must be given cautiously if a cat is being continually sick. Dehydration is a serious condition and the underlying cause should always be investigated so that appropriate treatment can be given. A seriously dehydrated cat may need to be hospitalized and given fluids intravenously in order to save its life.

dermatitis *see* ECZEMA.

dew claws vestigial thumbs that are situated on the inside of the front limbs above the paws. These claws may need to be trimmed in an elderly or ill cat that is not able to wear them down naturally.

diabetes mellitus a complex disorder that is rare in cats but where it does occur it affects middle-aged or elderly cats and is the result of a failure in the mechanism of sugar metabolism. It results in an accumulation of sugar in the blood and urine and is caused by a lack of the hormone insulin, which is secreted by cells in the pancreas. Symptoms include an excessive thirst and passing copious quantities of urine, which, when analysed, is found to contain sugar. The appetite increases greatly at first, but the cat loses weight gradually. Eventually, if the condition remains untreated, the cat becomes obviously ill. There is a loss of appetite, VOMITING, DEHYDRATION, lethargy and a typical 'pear drops' smell on the breath and from the urine resulting from the presence of substances called ketones. The cat passes into a diabetic COMA as a result of the metabolic crisis caused by excessively high levels of blood sugar. In this emergency condition, a cat requires immediate veterinary treatment in order for its life to be saved.

Diabetes in cats (and dogs) can only be treated by daily injections of insulin, which obviously requires considerable commitment from the owner. Depending upon individual circumstances it may, in fact, be kinder to have the cat humanely put to sleep. In treating a diabetic cat, one problem that can occasionally arise is giving an accidental overdose of insulin. The symptoms of this are disorientation, staggering, confused behaviour, convulsions and coma leading to death, caused by a sudden reduction in blood sugar. This is also an emergency that must be immediately remedied by giving the cat sugar in the form of honey, syrup or prepared glucose solution, which must be kept readily to hand. An owner who has reason to suspect the development of diabetes in a cat should seek immediate veterinary advice so that treatment can begin as soon as possible.

diagnostic tests as in human medicine, a veterinary surgeon may occasionally think it advisable to carry out certain investigative procedures on a cat in order to obtain a precise diagnosis of a particular problem. Depending upon the nature of the symptoms, a variety of tests could be carried out. These include analysis of samples of blood, urine, faeces, swabs of discharges that may be cultured for bacterial growth, ultrasound tests and exploratory surgery, particularly to carry out a biopsy of suspect tissue such as a TUMOUR. More complicated tests may sometimes be helpful, but no procedures are carried out without full consultation with, and the consent of, the cat's owners. Any investigation that might cause pain or distress is carried out under general ANAESTHETIC.

diarrhoea increased frequency and looseness of bowel movements involving the passage of unusually soft or watery faeces. In cats, as in humans, diarrhoea can have a number of different causes such as a dietary upset (excessive intake or eating an unsuitable, unusual or irritating substance). Other causes include bacterial or viral infections such as FELINE INFECTIOUS ENTERITIS, COCCIDIOSIS (protozoal infection) and infestation by certain internal parasites, particularly roundworms in kittens (*see also* PARASITES—Internal Parasites, page 128).

Diarrhoea in young kittens is always a cause for concern and requires immediate veterinary attention. In adult cats, as long as the animal otherwise appears to be well, treatment can first be given at home. All food should be withdrawn for a period of twenty-four hours and only water offered. After this time, a small quantity of light food such as steamed fish or chicken can be given to the cat, gradually returning to a normal diet as long as the diarrhoea does not return. If there is no improvement in the condition of the cat, consult a veterinary surgeon straight away.

dislocation the displacement of one of the two bones that form a joint from its normal position. Common sites are the hip, lower jaw and knee (stifle joint). A dislocation usually occurs as a result of an accidental blow where considerable force has been applied, and in cats it is often caused by a fall or being struck by a car. The hip may be dislocated as a result of a heavy landing following a jump and, characteristically, one hind leg appears to be shorter than the other. If the lower jaw is involved, the cat cannot close its mouth properly and its teeth are clearly not in the right position. In the case of the knee joint, the patella (knee cap) moves from its normal position and the cat walks in a stiff-legged fashion. This is usually a congenital defect, allowing the dislocation to occur without the application of undue force and especially affects cats of the Devon Rex breed. The characteristic symptoms of dislocation are pain and swelling around the affected joint so that the animal is unable to function normally.

In many instances, especially following an accident, it may be impossible to tell whether a fracture or a dislocation has occurred. A dislocation prevents movement at the joint but there are no broken bones and no bleeding. If a dislocation is suspected, keep the animal as quiet and still as possible and place it in a cat carrier or large cardboard box. Do not give it anything to eat or drink and take it immediately to a veterinary surgery. A general ANAESTHETIC is needed so that the joint can be restored to normal without further pain. Manipulation of bones is a skilled procedure that should only be carried out by a veterinary surgeon. Clumsy handling of a dislocated joint, or a delay in seeking treatment, may cause further damage and prevent or compromise healing.

ear inflammation (otitis externa) irritation, scratching and inflammation of the ear canal, possibly with a smelly, sticky discharge. The commonest cause is the presence of ear mites (*see* PARASITES—External Parasites, page 136). Another possible cause, especially in elderly cats, is a TUMOUR that can sometimes be malignant (*see* CANCER).

eclampsia ('milk fever', puerperal tetany) a serious condition that can arise in a queen cat shortly after giving birth to kittens. It is caused by a deficiency in calcium, a great deal of which is used during pregnancy to form the skeletal structure of the kittens and after birth in milk production. Eclampsia cannot be prevented from developing, and the best that can be done is to ensure that a pregnant and nursing queen receives plenty of good nourishing food containing calcium. (*See also* SEXUAL BEHAVIOUR AND BREEDING—Routine Care of a Queen Cat and Her Kittens, page 115.)

eczema and **dermatitis** inflamed and irritated skin that is itchy and may 'weep' but without any apparent cause such as the presence of external parasites. It is thought to be an allergic response, and the main problem is the self-inflicted damage to the skin caused by the cat's scratching. It is now believed that the most common cause is a hypersensitive response by certain cats to flea saliva. Such a cat reacts with severe itching to just a single flea bite and this condition is known as miliary eczema or miliary dermatitis. It is, of course, extremely important to protect an ALLERGIC cat from being bitten by fleas by using one of the insecticidal preparations that are available.

electrocardiogram (ECG) a record of the changes in the heart's electrical activity that is obtained by means of an instrument called an electrocardiograph. This is a type of DIAGNOSTIC TEST that may occasionally be recommended for a cat with a suspected heart disorder.

electroencephalogram (EEG) a record of the brain's electrical activity that is obtained by means of an instrument called an electroencephalograph. This type of recording may occasionally be useful in diagnosing brain disorders in cats.

Elizabethan collar a bucket-shaped device, looking rather like a lampshade, that is fitted over a cat's head to prevent it from scratching a sore ear or biting and interfering with a WOUND or bandage on some other part of its body. An Elizabethan collar can be obtained ready-made from a veterinary clinic or pet shop, but one can also be improvised at home. A children's sand bucket or a large flowerpot with the base cut out is often suitable as long as it is made from soft plastic that will 'give' a little. The edge that goes around the neck should be padded with sticking plaster to soften it, and strings fastened on to tie it to the cat's collar.

Another alternative is to make the collar from a piece of strong card bent into a cone shape and trimmed to size. The collar should not be so wide that it prevents the cat from lying down and must be removed to enable the animal to eat and drink. The cat should not be allowed to roam freely while wearing the collar in case it gets caught up in some way. The neck must be checked regularly for rubbing and more padding applied if necessary.

An Elizabethan collar

encephalitis inflammation of the brain, which is a rare condition in cats and usually associated with some infectious illness such as RABIES.

entamoebiasis a rare disease, caused by parasitic protozoa, that may occasionally affect cats in some countries of the world.

entropion an eye condition, seen particularly in some breeds such as Persians, in which one or both of the eyelids curl inwards and cause inflammation and irritation by rubbing on the eyeball. Corrective eye surgery is needed to remedy this condition.

epiphora the condition in which there are two wet streaks running from each eye down the side of the nose because of an overflow of tears (lacrimal fluid). In white cats, it produces a characteristic reddish-brown stain. Lacrimal fluid is continually produced by tear glands in the eyes and is washed across the surface by the action of blinking. Normally the excess drains away through the nasolacrimal duct that runs from the eye into the nasal cavity. In some cats, however, especially pedigree breeds with flat faces, e.g. Persians, the ducts may become blocked, and this results in tears flowing down the face. It may also occur in a cat with an eye inflammation or respiratory illness.

euthanasia there are occasions when the kindest and most responsible course of action is to have a cat put painlessly to sleep. Medically, this is only carried out when the cat's quality of life is poor and deteriorating and there is no hope of recovery. The usual method is by an injection of an overdose of ANAESTHETIC. The cat passes immediately into unconsciousness and a painless death.

eye worm (*Thelazia californiensis*) a parasitic worm that can affect rural cats in the southwest USA. The larval stage is transmitted by the deer fly, which inhabits woodland areas, and the worm develops behind the haw (third eyelid) of the cat. It causes a painful CONJUNCTIVITIS, and the only form of treatment is surgical removal of the parasite.

false pregnancy *see* SEXUAL BEHAVIOUR AND BREEDING, page 99.

feline calicivirus disease (**FCD**) one of the two main forms of FELINE RESPIRATORY DISEASE, or cat influenza, caused by feline caliciriviruses (FCV). On the whole, these viruses produce a milder form of the illness but this is not necessarily the case. Symptoms of FCD are sneezing, running eyes and nose, raised temperature, COUGHING and, characteristically, ULCERS in the mouth on the tongue and palate. Sometimes the symptoms are so mild as to pass unnoticed and usually a cat with this form of 'flu will make a good recovery. The viruses are highly contagious and are spread by direct contact from cat to cat. The virus is expelled when the cat sneezes or coughs and can also be picked up from bedding, etc, although it can survive for only about ten days in a normal environment. In kennels or a cattery, it is necessary to isolate the cat and carry out a rigorous cleaning programme using strong bleaches. Veterinary advice should be sought for any cat that displays symptoms of cat 'flu. Fortunately, infection with FCV can be prevented by vaccination.

feline infectious anaemia (feline haemobartonellosis) an infectious disease that is caused by the bacterium *Haemobartonella felis*. Many cats are believed to harbour the organism without showing signs of illness. It is most common in young tom cats and usually strikes during the spring and summer months. This is the time when there is more sexual activity and males are actively involved in fighting and trying to achieve dominance. Hence, it is likely that the organism is transmitted from one cat to another via infected saliva. Also, fleas probably spread the bacteria as they pass from one cat to another, and it is believed that the organism can cross the placenta to developing kittens during pregnancy.

The bacteria enter red blood cells and multiply rapidly, eventually causing rupture (haemolysis). New bacteria are then able to invade more red blood cells and there is further destruction. The bone marrow cannot replace the lost cells fast enough, so the typical symptom is (haemolytic) ANAEMIA with pallor of mucous membranes, lethargy and loss of appetite. A cat displaying these symptoms should be taken to a veterinary surgeon and microscopic examination of a blood sample reveals the presence of the bacteria. Treatment is by means of courses of antibiotics, but severely anaemic cats may need a blood transfusion.

feline infectious enteritis (feline virus enteritis, feline panleucopenia) a serious and highly contagious viral disease of cats that is common in all parts of the world. Cats become infected either through direct contact or indirectly via objects, such as bedding, that have become contaminated. The virus, of a type known as a parvovirus, is a long-lasting one that can persist in the environment for over a year and is extremely resistant to decay. It can be destroyed by using certain strong bleaches and by boiling, but it is difficult to be certain that it has been eradicated. Symptoms usually appear about five to ten days after infection, beginning with VOMITING, apathy, high temperature and DIARRHOEA. There is severe abdominal pain and thirst, and the cat may sit hunched up near its water bowl but is too ill and miserable to attempt to drink. The animal quickly becomes DEHYDRATED and may collapse and die quite quickly within five days of first showing symptoms. The outlook for kittens under three months of age is usually poor. A veterinary surgeon should be consulted immediately if a cat is showing any signs of this illness. The animal may need to be hospitalized, kept in isolation and given fluids intravenously and will also be prescribed antibiotics to deal with any secondary bacterial infections. There are no drugs available to kill the virus so treatment is aimed at relieving symptoms. The virus causes a reduction in the cat's white blood cell count, and some animals may need a blood transfusion. Unfortunately, even those cats that recover may have sustained residual damage to their intestine and bowel and be prone to diarrhoea. If a pregnant queen cat becomes infected she may abort the foetuses or the virus may cause brain damage in the kittens that becomes apparent only after birth. Since the virus persists for so long in the environment, other animals should be kept away from affected premises for at least six months. Fortunately, this unpleasant and distressing disease can be prevented by vaccination.

feline infectious peritonitis (FIP) a viral disease of cats that was first identified about 35 years ago and the incidence of which appears to be increasing. It is more common in young animals under three years old and those living in groups. It is believed that many more cats are infected than the number showing signs of illness and that most (80 per cent) develop a natural immunity. Often, FIP seems to flare up in a cat that is already suffering from FELINE LEUKAEMIA, presumably because of the animal's compromised immunity.

FIP produces two sets of symptoms, only one of which features peritonitis or inflammation of the peritoneum, the serous membrane that lines the abdominal cavity. In both forms of the illness, the incubation period is weeks or even months after initial infection. Symptoms are similar at first and include loss of appetite and weight, raised temperature and DEHYDRATION. In the 'wet' form, fluid collects in the abdomen (ASCITES) and frequently in the chest cavity, causing BREATHING PROBLEMS. There is accompanying peritonitis. In the 'dry' form, oedema (fluid collection) is absent but there may be damage to the kidneys and nervous tissue. The eyes are also affected and may undergo a colour change.

Unfortunately, there is no cure for this illness, and the most that can be done is to try to relieve the symptoms. There is a high mortality rate, death usually occurring two to five weeks after the symptoms have first appeared.

feline leukaemia a common disease of cats, caused by a virus, that has been designated feline leukaemia virus or FeLV. In fact, it is not strictly comparable to the leukaemia that affects people (and dogs), taking a somewhat different form and having an identifiable cause, a virus that can be readily transmitted to other cats. The virus commonly causes CANCER in the form of malignant TUMOURS, known as lymphomas, that arise in lymph tissue of the lymph nodes, spleen and thymus gland and also the kidneys, nasal passages and nervous system. Symptoms are variable depending upon the site of the tumour but include loss of appetite and weight, feverishness, BREATHING PROBLEMS, swallowing difficulties, DIARRHOEA and ANAEMIA. Anaemia occurs because the virus may damage both the immune system and the bone marrow and red blood cells. Compromised immunity enables other illnesses to gain a hold, particularly FELINE INFECTIOUS ANAEMIA and FELINE INFECTIOUS PERITONITIS. Infections of the mouth and gums (GINGIVITIS) also may occur because of lowered immunity.

A cat showing any symptoms of illness should be taken to a veterinary surgeon. Diagnosis is made through analysis of samples. Unfortunately, there is no cure and over two thirds of cats with leukaemia die within one or two years. Symptoms can be relieved with palliative drug treatment. Recently a vaccine has been developed to protect cats against this severe disease and so it is hoped the incidence will decline.

feline pneumonitis an infectious illness affecting cats in parts of the USA and caused by *Chlamydia* bacteria. These organisms may also contribute in a minor way in some cases of FELINE RESPIRATORY DISEASE.

feline reovirus infection reoviruses are a group that occasionally cause a very minor form of FELINE RESPIRATORY DISEASE, mainly in the form of CONJUNCTIVITIS, but this is considered to be relatively insignificant. They can infect cats and other animals in another way, causing the disease PSEUDORABIES.

feline salmonellosis an uncommon but highly infectious form of gastroenteritis in cats characterized by VOMITING, DIARRHOEA containing blood and high temperature. It is possible for this illness to be passed from a cat to a person although this is believed to be rare.

feline urological syndrome (**FUS**) a serious disorder affecting male cats in which particles of crystalline material build up to form a blockage of the urethra (the duct carrying urine from the bladder to the outside via the penis). The cat repeatedly licks his penis and makes frequent visits to the litter tray but passes little or no urine. Any that is passed may be tinged with blood. The posture of the cat is noticeably different from normal—his back is arched and the head lowered and the whole body is tensed, indicative of pain.

The cat may cry out and is evidently in pain. He should be taken immediately to a veterinary surgeon and not given any food or drink. Usually a general ANAESTHETIC is needed in order to pass a catheter into the bladder to remove the blockage and withdraw urine. Sometimes the urine has to be taken off by means of a needle that is introduced into the bladder through the wall of the abdomen. Occasionally abdominal surgery is needed. There should be no delay in seeking treatment if FUS is suspected, as the condition can worsen rapidly leading to SHOCK and death. Rarely, a cat may even burst its bladder or the kidneys may be affected, causing worsening renal failure.

Feline urological syndrome frequently recurs, and a cat that has had such a problem should not be given dried foods that have been implicated in its development. Female cats do not get FUS as they possess a wider urethra and normally pass any 'grit' without difficulty.

Signs and symptons of feline urological virus

licking the opening of the urethra

strained posture

hunched posture—back is arched and muscles are tensed

appears distressed and may emit a cry

front legs are vertical

hind legs are also held more vertically

feline viral rhinotracheitis (FVR infection) feline viral rhinotracheitis virus causes the most severe of the two forms of FE-
LINE RESPIRATORY DISEASE or cat influenza. The illness is passed
by direct and indirect contact (with infected bedding, etc) and
is particularly dangerous where many cats are kept together.
Symptoms appear after about ten days following infection and
include runny eyes and nose, sneezing, profuse salivation,
COUGHING, loss of appetite, feverishness and apathy. Secondary
bacterial infections are common, and the discharges may become thick and purulent, causing BREATHING PROBLEMS and eyes
that are gummed together. ULCERS in the mouth and eyes may
develop. After about one week, most cats usually begin to improve but the main problem is persuading them to eat and
drink. DEHYDRATION is a very real danger, and when deaths occur (particularly in elderly cats and kittens) they are usually either due to this or to the development of PNEUMONIA. Hence it is
vital to take a cat displaying any symptoms for veterinary treatment, which takes the form of antibiotics to combat secondary
infection and, in severe cases, intravenous fluid replacement.
Some cats that recover are left with persistent catarrh and
breathing problems that, rarely, may affect the sinuses within
the skull. Fortunately, vaccination (*see* GROOMING AND CARE—
Vaccination, page 72) can prevent this unpleasant disease and
is particularly important since recovered cats are generally car-
riers of the virus. Also, FVR virus is believed to be unable to

fits

survive for more than one day away from a cat and is readily destroyed by disinfectants and bleaches. Devoted nursing of a cat with this illness is of great benefit in making the animal feel better and speeding up its recovery.

fits *see* CONVULSIONS.

foreign body (in the mouth or swallowed) kittens and juvenile cats may pick up some inappropriate and indigestible object in their mouth during play, and this may become stuck or may be swallowed. Cats that are in the habit of eating their prey may have problems with a bone becoming caught behind the teeth. It is usually fairly obvious if something is stuck in a cat's mouth by the chewing movements of its jaws and tongue. The cat paws at its mouth and often produces lots of saliva in its attempts to dislodge the object. If there is any obstruction of the airway, the cat will make choking noises (*see* A-Z OF FIRST AID FOR CATS, page 235). If the cat's efforts are unsuccessful, try to remove the object yourself. Wrap the cat up in a thick towel so that only its head is free and place it on a table. It is easier if there are two people, one of whom firmly restrains the cat. Take hold of the scruff (the loose skin at the back of the neck) and turn the cat's head to the side so that its nose points towards the ceiling. Usually the mouth opens at the same time but, if not, the lower jaw can be pulled downwards gently. If possible, remove the object using tweezers or thin pliers to avoid the risk of being bitten.

A swallowed object may sometimes pass through the gut and be eliminated with the faeces without causing harm, but unfortunately this is not always the case. An object may become stuck or cause an obstruction or perforation in some part of the gut with serious consequences. It may get as far as the rectum and become lodged there, causing the cat to strain and lick the anal area. If there is any reason to suspect that a cat has swallowed some object it is wise to consult a veterinary surgeon without delay. The cat may need to have X-rays to locate the object and surgery to remove it, carried out under a general ANAESTHETIC.

fracture any break in a bone that may be complete or incomplete. In a simple (or closed) fracture, the skin remains more or less intact but in a compound (or open) fracture there is an open wound connecting the broken bone with the surface. This type of fracture is generally more serious as it provides a greater risk of infection and more blood loss. A 'greenstick' fracture occurs in a young animal whose bones are still soft and tend to bend rather than break. The fracture occurs on the opposite side to the causal force. A complicated fracture involves damage to surrounding soft tissue, including nerves and blood vessels. A depressed fracture involves the skull when a piece of bone is forced inwards and may damage the brain.

Fractures are frequent injuries in cats, generally as a result of a road accident. The commonest bones involved are the femur (thigh) of the hind limbs, the pelvis, lower jaw and tail. It can be difficult to determine whether a cat has suffered a fracture or a DISLOCATION, and diagnostic X-rays may be needed. Certain symptoms and signs of a fracture may be present. These include severe pain and swelling, an unusual degree of movement with a grating sound (crepitus), or there may be an obvious bump where a broken bone has been displaced. The pain and bleeding that may result from a fracture can easily lead to SHOCK, and the cat requires immediate veterinary treatment. It will normally need surgery under general anaesthetic to repair the damage. Emergency treatment of broken bones and dislocations is discussed in the A-Z OF FIRST AID FOR CATS, which begins on page 225.

frostbite a rare condition in cats, and when it does occur it usually affects the tips of the ears, which appear to be white and cold and to lack sensation. Veterinary advice should be obtained in cases of suspected frostbite, but, as an interim measure warm, *but not hot*, pads can be applied to the affected parts. As the circulation returns to normal, the skin usually reddens and is painful for a time. If the skin turns black rather than red (indicating GANGRENE) take the cat to a veterinary surgeon immediately.

fur balls or **hairballs** cylindrical 'bullets' of accumulated fur that form from the hairs that are swallowed by a cat during grooming. They are particularly likely to occur in long-haired cats and are usually VOMITED up without causing harm. Sometimes, however, they may cause a blockage in the intestine, which may necessitate surgical removal under general ANAESTHETIC.

gangrene the death of tissue because of a loss of blood supply or bacterial infection. There are two types of gangrene, 'dry' and 'moist'. Dry gangrene is caused purely by a loss of blood supply, and the affected part becomes cold and then turns brown or black. There is an obvious line of demarcation between living and dead tissue, and eventually the gangrenous part is sloughed off. Moist gangrene is caused by bacterial infection and there is putrefaction and fluid leakage with an obnoxious smell. There is pain and fever, and without prompt surgical intervention and antibiotic treatment, bacterial toxins are absorbed into the bloodstream, leading to death from blood poisoning. Gangrene can occur in a cat as a result of injury, BURNS, FROSTBITE, etc, and is obviously more likely if suitable treatment for a WOUND is delayed or in a stray or neglected animal. It is always best to seek veterinary advice about the treatment of a wound or injury, particularly since cats are prone to infections.

giardiasis a rare disease in cats (which can also occur in people), affecting the digestive system and caused by a parasitic protozoan microorganism.

gingivitis inflammation of the gums. This is usually caused by a buildup of tartar on the teeth at their junction with the gums, which enables bacteria to proliferate and attack the tissues. The gums become red, swollen and irritated and bleed easily. If the tartar is not removed at this stage, the situation worsens and the gums may continue to swell and pull away from the root of the teeth. Bacteria are then able to attack the socket of the teeth, causing them to become loose and leading to severe infection or abscesses and great pain. This condition is known as PERIODONTAL DISEASE. Gingivitis in cats can also occur with FELINE LEUKAEMIA and TRENCH MOUTH. (*See also* GROOMING AND CARE—Care of Teeth, page 68.)

glaucoma a painful disorder caused by pressure from a buildup of fluid within the eye, usually in elderly cats that have a CATARACT. Veterinary treatment is needed and specialized surgery may be required.

glomerulonephritis a kidney disease in cats that is often an auto-immune disorder, i.e. one in which the damage is caused by the immune system. The cat requires a diet that is very high in protein but unfortunately, the condition often progresses to KIDNEY FAILURE.

Griseofulvin an effective antifungal drug used in the treatment of RINGWORM.

haematoma a collection or leakage of blood that forms a firm swelling beneath the skin. It can arise anywhere as a result of a blow causing the rupture of a small blood vessel. In cats (and dogs), however, the most common site is the flap of an ear, arising as a result of a fight or head shaking and scratching caused by infestation with ear mites (*see* PARASITES—External Parasites, page 140). The haematoma appears as a swelling that may alter in shape and is uncomfortable but not severely painful. The cat should be taken to a veterinary surgeon, and usually the haematoma needs to be opened and drained under a general ANAESTHETIC. Otherwise there will be a permanent distortion or crumpled 'cauliflower' ear.

haemorrhage bleeding—a flow of blood from a ruptured blood vessel that may occur externally or internally. A haemorrhage is classified according to the type of vessels involved. Arterial haemorrhage is when bright red blood spurts in pulses from an artery. Venous haemorrhage is when there is a darker-coloured, steady flow from a vein. In a capillary haemorrhage, blood oozes from torn capillaries at the surface of a wound. In addition, a haemorrhage may be primary, i.e. it occurs at the moment of injury. A secondary haemorrhage can arise later as a result of infection (sepsis). Haemorrhage from a major artery is the most serious as large volumes of blood are quickly lost and death can occur within minutes. Haemorrhages at specific sites within the body are designated by special names, e.g. haematuria from the kidney or urinary tract, often indicated by the presence of blood in the urine. Also, haemoptysis, bleeding from the lungs, indicated by the coughing up of blood and haematemesis, from the digestive organs, which may be apparent if blood is VOMITED. (*See also* A-Z OF FIRST AID FOR CATS, page 227.)

hairballs *see* FUR BALLS.

halitosis *see* BAD BREATH.

haw (third eyelid) a protective membrane, called the 'nictitating membrane', that can be seen in the corner of the eye as a small pink mass. In a cat that is DEHYDRATED, debilitated or suffering from an irritative condition, the haws may be seen passing sideways across the eyes. It is best to report this to your veterinary surgeon in case the cat requires treatment.

heart disease in common with human beings, cats may suffer from heart disease, which tends to be more common in older age. The form this takes differs, however, in that cats nearly always suffer from increasing weakness and failure of the heart muscle (cardiomyopathy) rather than the 'furring' of the pulmonary arteries which is so common in people. In about half of all cats with this condition, blood clots are able to form within the chambers of the heart as blood flows more sluggishly. These are eventually carried away in the circulation, and often one lodges in the fork of the major artery that divides to supply each hind limb (aortic thromboembolism). The circulation to the limbs is severely reduced or cut off, and there is pain, coldness and a lack of pulse. The muscles are not able to work properly and the cat cannot use its hind legs. Unfortunately, this condition cannot be cured and may progress to heart failure.

heartworm (*Dirofilaria immitis*) internal parasites that occur uncommonly in cats in some parts of Europe, Australia and the USA. The larval stage of the parasite is transmitted from one infected animal to another via mosquito bites. Once in the bloodstream, larvae travel to the heart and pulmonary artery which connects with the lungs. They develop into adult worms and cause a severe COUGH, BREATHING PROBLEMS and possibly even death.

heatstroke or **heat hyperpyrexia** a severe condition following exposure of a cat to excessive heat with a consequent rapid rise in its body temperature. It is more common in dogs, but a cat, if confined in a hot, poorly ventilated place with no access to water for a prolonged period, will eventually suffer heatstroke as its temperature regulation mechanisms are overcome. The circumstances in which this might occur are if the cat becomes accidentally trapped in a hot, stuffy shed, car, tumble-drier, airing cupboard, etc. The only mechanisms that the cat has to prevent overheating are seeking out shade, sweating through the paws, panting and drinking water. Symptoms of heatstroke are firstly panting, drooling and anxiety, and the gums turn a bright red colour. The temperature climbs rapidly above the normal 38.5°C, leading to COMA, respiratory collapse (blue tinge to gums) and death.

Heatstroke is an emergency that requires immediate action to lower the cat's temperature. It may be necessary to give artificial respiration (*see* A-Z OF FIRST AID FOR CATS, page 226). Place the animal in a bowl or sink full of cold water, supporting its head above the water. After five or ten minutes there should be an improvement and the cat should start to become more aware of its surroundings. Ideally, keep a check on the cat's rectal temperature and remove it from the water once this reaches 39.2°C. This is because the temperature will continue to *fall* for a time once it has been removed from the water. The temperature regulation mechanism has been disturbed, and it is possible to over-cool the cat. Dry the cat and offer it drinking water and keep it confined in cool surroundings while you seek veterinary advice. Sometimes, even after an apparent recovery, symptoms can begin again and it is important to keep a close eye on the cat. Cats should *never* be left in a car in warm or hot weather, even if the windows are open.

Flat-faced cats such as Persians and elderly and obese animals are more susceptible to heatstroke.

hernia the protrusion of a greater or lesser part of an organ from out of its normal position in the abdominal cavity because of a weakness or rupture in restraining sheets of muscle. A congenital hernia is present at birth, and the commonest one is an umbilical hernia in a newborn kitten. A part of the intestine bulges into the umbilicus, because of the failure of muscles beneath in the abdominal wall to close over. This can usually be corrected by surgery. An inguinal hernia is rare in cats but involves a portion of the bowel protruding through the inguinal canal in the lower abdomen or groin.

A potentially more serious type of hernia can follow an accidental blow when the muscles of the diaphragm tear or rupture. Loops of intestine are then able to bulge into the chest cavity, and this causes pain and distressed breathing. The cat is not able to lie down, and immediate corrective surgery is needed to repair the damage and save its life.

hyperthyroidism a rare disorder in cats resulting from excessive activity of the thyroid gland (an overactive thyroid), causing an increased production of hormones. One sign of this is an increased appetite but accompanied by a loss of weight.

hypothermia the bodily state in which a cat's core temperature falls below 36.7°C as a result of prolonged exposure to cold, wet conditions. At first, shivering occurs and the heart works harder to increase blood flow around the body. Eventually shivering ceases, however, and with increased chilling the function of the body organs becomes disturbed and cardiac output falls. The tissues require less oxygen as their functions start to fail, but eventually the heart is unable to supply even this reduced demand. The symptoms of hypothermia are shivering, then fatigue, lethargy, confusion, CONVULSIONS and COMA. The cat's breathing is very shallow and slow, and the body feels cold to the touch. Death follows unless the cat is warmed and its core temperature induced to rise.

Any cat can develop hypothermia if it is out in cold, wet and windy weather for a long time and cannot obtain shelter, particularly if it is injured or trapped and cannot move about. Young kittens, elderly cats and thin-coated breeds such as the Rex types are particularly vulnerable. Immediate first aid treatment is needed in the form of drying the cat and wrapping it in blankets and placing it in a warm room but not directly near a source of heat. It may be necessary to give emergency artificial respiration in some cases (*see* A-Z OF FIRST AID FOR CATS, page 226).

incontinence this may occur in the bladder or bowels in elderly cats and, depending upon the cause, may be difficult to treat successfully. Apparent urinary incontinence in younger male cats may, in fact, be an indication of FELINE UROLOGICAL SYNDROME.

Jacobson's organs *see* VOMERONASAL ORGANS.

jaundice a condition characterized by the unusual presence of bile pigment (bilirubin) in the blood, which is normally a symptom of LIVER DISEASE With jaundice, bile that is produced in the liver and stored in the gall bladder passes into the blood instead of the intestines, and because of this the skin and mucus membranes take on a yellowish appearance. This is noticed in the whites of the eyes and lining of the eyelids, tongue and gums. The urine also turns a strong yellow or brown colour because of the presence of the pigment. Possible causes include FELINE INFECTIOUS ANAEMIA, DIABETES MELLITUS, POISONING and liver TUMOUR. A jaundiced cat is evidently ill and normally shows other symptoms. Urgent veterinary treatment is essential.

kidney disease there are two common forms in cats, GLOMERULONEPHRITIS, which is an immune system disorder, and progressive kidney failure, which may occur as a natural degeneration in old age. Other possible contributory causes are lymphosarcoma (*see* CANCER), bacterial infection, and damage to the kidneys, usually sustained as a result of a road accident. The damage or degeneration of the kidneys means that they are no longer able efficiently to filter waste products from the blood. These toxic substances accumulate in the circulation and cause symptoms that include loss of appetite and weight, lethargy, VOMITING, extreme thirst, DEHYDRATION and eventually the development of painful mouth ULCERS.

Unfortunately, chronic kidney failure cannot be reversed and, while the symptoms can sometimes be relieved by feeding a *low* protein diet and with drugs, it may be necessary to have the cat put humanely to sleep. Acute kidney failure, producing similar symptoms but arising suddenly in cats of younger age caused by, e.g. POISONING, accidental damage, FELINE UROLOGICAL SYNDROME or dehydration, are often temporary and respond to treatment, but these cats may be more likely to develop the chronic form in old age. Leptospirosis, which is often responsible for kidney disease in dogs, is virtually unknown in cats.

lameness cats are much less susceptible than dogs to strains and sprains of the limbs, although ARTHRITIS can be a cause of lameness in elderly animals. A more frequent cause of lameness in cats (apart from accidental injury) is a septic BITE or ABSCESS on some part of a limb.

laparotomy a general term for a surgical procedure in which

an incision is made into the abdomen under general ANAES-
THETIC. Sometimes an instrument is inserted in order to obtain a
sample of tissue for laboratory investigation (*see* BIOPSY). A
laparotomy is also necessary for various abdominal operations
such as NEUTERING of a female cat.

leprosy feline leprosy is a rare condition but one that is quite
widespread and is caused by a bacterium similar to the TUBER-
CULOSIS organism. It causes small raised lumps to appear on the
skin and these may develop into ULCERS. The condition requires
veterinary treatment with antibiotic drugs.

lick granuloma a thickness of shiny tissue that can occur over
the surface of a wound that has not been able to heal properly
because of a cat's continual licking. It is important to try to prevent a cat from licking a wound as this delays and interrupts
healing, may dislodge stitches and result in the formation of a
thickened mass of scar tissue. In cats, lick granulomas can occur as a result of the animal's excessive grooming, usually on
the under-surface or inner thighs. The lesions require veterinary treatment, and it may be necessary to prevent the cat from
licking itself by fitting it with an ELIZABETHAN COLLAR.

listeriosis a chronic bacterial infection that may rarely occur
in cats, producing a range of symptoms.

liver disease or **damage** is relatively uncommon in cats and produces a variety of symptoms, including DIARRHOEA and VOMITING, loss of appetite and weight, abdominal swelling as a result of fluid accumulation and JAUNDICE. Liver disorder may be a feature of several conditions, including FELINE INFECTIOUS ANAEMIA and DIABETES MELLITUS. The cat needs expert veterinary care as it is more vulnerable than usual to the effects of drugs, which must be given very cautiously.

lung fluke an internal parasite of some cats in parts of South Africa and the USA. This parasite, *Paragonimus kellicotti*, has larval stages in crayfish and water snails. It usually infests stray cats that scavenge on shorelines and causes COUGHING and irritation of the airways.

mastitis inflammation of one or two mammary glands in a nursing queen cat (*see* SEXUAL BEHAVIOUR AND BREEDING—Routine Care of a Queen Cat and Her Kittens, page 115).

meningitis inflammation of the meninges (membranes) surrounding the brain and spinal cord. It is rare in cats.

metritis inflammation and infection of the womb, which may arise in a queen cat following the birth of her kittens. This is a potentially severe and life-threatening condition, producing symptoms of loss of appetite, lethargy, lack of interest in caring for the kittens, high temperature and a foul-smelling discharge that may be bloodstained. The cat requires urgent veterinary treatment with antibiotics to kill the infection. (*See also* SEXUAL BEHAVIOUR AND BREEDING—Labour and Birth, page 108.)

mouse favus a type of RINGWORM that normally affects rodents and for which a cat can be a carrier without displaying symptoms. It may be possible for this to be passed via cats to human beings.

mycetoma a rare fungal infection that may affect cats in certain parts of the USA and causes COUGHING, fever and loss of weight.

mycoplasma bacteria that may be implicated in a minor way in some cases of FELINE RESPIRATORY DISEASE and may occasionally be involved in spontaneous abortion in pregnant queen cats.

neutering a surgical operation to remove the reproductive organs of a cat to prevent mating and breeding. In tom cats this operation, also known as castration or orchidectomy, involves the removal of the testicles. In queen cats, ovariohysterectomy, or spaying, involves the removal of the womb and ovaries. Since the reproductive organs are completely removed, the sex hormones that they secrete and that are responsible for sexual behaviour are no longer present, and this modifies the cat's behaviour. In both sexes, this normally means that the animal no longer shows any sexual interest, although occasionally, in an older male cat, mating behaviour may have become conditioned and persist for a time.

Neutering generally prevents the habit of urine spraying by males and is almost completely effective if the operation is carried out before puberty. Occasionally it may persist in an older male in whom it has become ingrained behaviour. A queen cat no longer comes into oestrus, so calling ceases. Neutered cats are more likely to become obese, but this tendency is readily controlled by adjusting food intake. (*See also* Sexual Behaviour and Breeding, page 92.)

nocardiosis a rare bacterial infection of cats that affects the lungs and causes BREATHING PROBLEMS.

nystagmus involuntary, rapid eye movements in which the pupils flick from side to side. In cats, it generally results from concussion after an accidental blow on the head or is a symptom of a middle ear infection.

obesity *see* DIET—Overfeeding and Obesity, page 48.

oedema an accumulation of fluid in the body, possibly beneath the skin or in cavities or organs. In the case of an injury, the swelling may be localized, but fluid accumulation can be more general, as in LIVER DISEASE. Other similar terms that may be used are ASCITES and 'dropsy'.

orthopaedic surgery orthopaedic surgery to repair FRACTURES is quite commonly performed on cats. Often, long bones in the limbs may be secured with metal surgical pins or plates, while wire is frequently used to repair a broken jaw.

otitis externa a scientific name for CANKER, meaning any infection and inflammation of the external ear canal.

paralysis a condition ranging from muscle weakness to total loss of muscle movement and sensation caused by disease or damage to the brain, spinal cord or an individual nerve pathway. A cat may suffer paralysis of a front limb as a result of an accidental injury that damages the radial nerve. This is called 'radial paralysis' and is caused by a severe blow on the shoulder, often a glancing knock from a car. There is a complete loss of sensation in the affected limb, which is dragged along the ground and is liable to suffer further damage. If the nerve is badly damaged and unlikely to recover, the only solution is amputation of the limb, which will otherwise become GANGRE-NOUS. Although this looks ungainly, most cats are adaptable and manage well on three legs if they have to.

The long tail of a cat is susceptible to similar paralysis if it becomes severely damaged in an accident. Once again, amputation is a very successful form of treatment, and a cat can manage quite happily with part of its tail or none at all.

Posterior paralysis, affecting the hind quarters and back legs, is a relatively common occurrence in cats as a result of spinal injuries sustained in road accidents. As well as losing all sensation and movement, the cat is often doubly incontinent as well. Sadly, there is usually little prospect of recovery, and the kindest course of action may be to have the cat put painlessly to sleep.

periodontal disease severe inflammation and disease of the gums, usually resulting from a buildup of tartar on the teeth (*see* GINGIVITIS and GROOMING AND CARE—Care of Teeth, page 68).

plaster casts a cat that FRACTURES the lower part of a limb may need to have the leg immobilized in plaster while the bone heals. Plaster casts are not an ideal solution for cats as they tend to get wet, chewed or dislodged in some way. Modern synthetic materials can be used and have many advantages, including lighter weight and increased durability, but the cost of these may prove prohibitive.

pleurisy inflammation of the pleura, the membranes that cover the lungs and line the inside of the chest wall. It is a severe and painful condition that can prove difficult to treat and may be fatal. It usually arises as a result of infection and may be a complication of FELINE RESPIRATORY DISEASE, FELINE INFECTIOUS PERITONITIS and FELINE LEUKAEMIA. Symptoms include rapid, laboured breathing, high temperature and the inability to lie because of severe pain and breathing difficulties. The condition can arise quite suddenly and requires urgent veterinary treatment.

pneumonia an infection of the lungs resulting in inflammation with the small air sacs becoming filled with pus and fluid. In cats, it usually arises as a result of a secondary bacterial infection as a complication of FELINE RESPIRATORY DISEASE. The symptoms are BREATHING PROBLEMS, fever and loss of appetite. The cat needs veterinary treatment with antibiotics and should be kept indoors in warm surroundings.

poisoning cats are relatively less likely to consume poisonous substances than dogs as they are more fastidious about what they eat. However, cases of poisoning certainly do occur in cats, either through directly eating the substance itself, consuming a prey animal that has been poisoned or licking and swallowing a toxic substance from the fur. Cats are more vulnerable to the effects of poisoning than some other species as the liver is relatively poor in its ability to detoxify these substances. Some substances, especially those containing phenol, can be absorbed through the skin but cases of inhalation of toxic fumes are uncommon.

Symptoms of poisoning vary according to the type of substance involved. Corrosive substances such as some household and DIY chemicals (acids and alkalis, fluids containing lysol or phenol, paint strippers, fuel oils, oven cleaner, caustic soda, etc) cause BURNS and BLISTERS in and around the mouth, internal burns, fluid loss and SHOCK. Some of these substances, particularly phenol, lysol and white spirit, can be absorbed through the skin. These substances are very dangerous, and it may be necessary to give emergency artificial respiration and cardiopulmonary resuscitation (*see* A-Z OF FIRST AID FOR CATS, pages 226, 234).

If there is reason to suspect that a cat has been poisoned with a corrosive poison and the animal is conscious, wash the mouth with plenty of cool, clean water. In addition, trickle water into the mouth by means of a teaspoon or syringe. Do not attempt to induce VOMITING as the substance causes more burning as it is brought back up, but dilute it with water as far as possible. Take the cat immediately to a veterinary clinic.

If the cat's coat is contaminated with a poisonous substance (commonly paint, road tar or fuel oil such as petrol or diesel) *never* attempt to remove it with any form of white spirit, strong detergent or disinfectant. If a small area is involved, cut off the affected hair and wash the area with plenty of warm water and mild shampoo. If a large area is affected, rub in a good quantity of vegetable oil, margarine, butter or lard to soften the substance, and wrap the cat in a towel. If the substance has hardened, you may have to wait for several hours for softening to occur, and the cat must be kept under constant supervision to prevent grooming. It is sensible to obtain veterinary advice. Later, bath the cat using plenty of warm water and mild shampoo and continue until all traces of the substance are removed.

With *known* ingested poisons other than corrosive substances, induce vomiting only if the animal is *fully* conscious. It is best to use a small knob of washing soda about the size of a marble or some crystals of rock salt. Alternatively, a strong solution of half a tablespoon of salt in a little warm water administered by syringe can be given. Wrap a towel around the cat to restrain it and place one hand around the head, face and upper jaw from behind. Raise the head upwards, holding the jaw to open the mouth and introduce the substance. Place it at the back of the tongue and close the mouth, keeping the head raised. Stroking the underside of the throat induces swallowing. Vomiting normally occurs within ten minutes or a quarter of an hour, and in the meantime obtain veterinary advice. Do not repeat the process if the cat does not vomit but take it to a veterinary clinic straight away.

Symptoms caused by ingested poisons include abdominal pain, DIARRHOEA, VOMITING, BREATHING PROBLEMS, neurological symptoms, CONVULSIONS, PARALYSIS, listlessness, COMA and collapse (SHOCK). All these are sufficiently serious to warrant emergency veterinary treatment even if one cannot be sure that poisoning is the cause. If the poison is known, take the container it came in or any other information about it with you to the veterinary surgeon as this will be of value in giving treatment to counteract its effects.

Of course, the best way to prevent incidents of poisoning is to play it safe at all times by keeping toxic substances well out of a cat's way. Some cats develop a perverse liking for substances, such as antifreeze, that are poisonous. Remember that some of the medicines that can be given to people and dogs are highly toxic to cats so never leave any of these lying around. Aspirin and paracetamol, commonly used in the home, are both in this category. Make sure that any veterinary products you use are suitable for your cat, and stick rigidly to dosing guidelines. Take particular care with insecticidal preparations, which can easily prove toxic if amounts are exceeded. Finally, discourage your cat from chewing house and garden plants, which may be poisonous, but make sure it has access to grass.

prolapse a situation in which a part of an organ protrudes down through a natural body aperture. In cats, this occasionally affects the rectum, following severe DIARRHOEA, or the uterus after the birth of kittens. The cat requires immediate veterinary treatment, usually in the form of corrective surgery, so it should not be given anything to eat or drink.

protozoal diseases diseases that can affect cats (and other mammals) and are caused by microorganisms called protozoa. The most important one in cats is TOXOPLASMOSIS.

pseudopregnancy *see* SEXUAL BEHAVIOUR AND BREEDING, page 99.

pseudorabies (Aujesky's disease) an unpleasant viral disease that occurs in most parts of the world, although it is absent from the UK and Australia. Cats are thought to contract the virus by eating infected rats, and the illness is short, intense and usually fatal. The cat becomes highly excited, mews excessively and froths at the mouth as a result of excessive salivation. It develops a severe itch and scratches constantly, making the skin raw and bleeding. This is called 'mad itch', which is another popular name for this illness. Following this, the animal becomes lethargic, loses coordination and becomes progressively PARALYSED, lapsing into COMA and death. There is a superficial resemblance to RABIES, but it is of shorter duration and unpredictable attacks on other animals are not a feature of the illness.

pseudotuberculosis a bacterial infection that rarely affects cats.

pyometra inflammation and infection of the womb, leading to a buildup of pus, which is an uncommon condition in female cats. Symptoms include a vaginal discharge, lethargy, thirst, high temperature, loss of appetite and VOMITING. The cat requires urgent veterinary treatment, normally in the form of surgery to remove the womb (NEUTERING), along with courses of antibiotics.

rabies an extremely severe viral disease that can affect people, cats, dogs and many other wild and domestic animals. Once symptoms are present, it is invariably fatal except in the case of one or two extremely rare exceptions. The normal route of transmission is through the BITE of an infected (rabid) animal, the virus being present in saliva. It is possible, although unlikely, for saliva to enter through an existing cut or to be inhaled.

Both people and cats can be vaccinated against rabies. However, vaccination is not permitted for pets in the UK except in special circumstances, i.e. if they are going into quarantine kennels or abroad to a country where rabies is endemic. In some countries, e.g. most parts of the USA, vaccination is a legal requirement for owners of cats and dogs.

The fate of a cat bitten by another animal that is proved to be rabid depends very much upon the country concerned and the vaccination status. The accepted recommendation is that a non-vaccinated animal should immediately be put to sleep. It may be possible for a vaccinated cat to be treated with antiserum or vaccination and then to be kept strictly quarantined for a period of at least three months. In western countries, it is rare for a person to be infected with rabies. Prompt treatment of any bite, by thorough cleansing of the wound and injections of the rabies vaccine, antiserum and immunoglobulin, can prevent the disease from developing. Tragically, those in other parts of the world are often not as fortunate.

A cat with rabies passes through three stages, and symptoms usually appear within one month, although it may be four months or longer. In the first stage (the prodromal), which is short-lived and lasts for two days or less, there is a change in the cat's nature. The animal usually becomes fearful and wishes to hide away or, less commonly, it is more affectionate than usual. The second stage is one of great excitement and agitation, called 'furious' rabies, which lasts longer in cats than in other animals. It may persist for up to four days, in which time the cat, if disturbed, attacks anything within reach, including objects, people and other animals. This occurs without warning and the cat hangs on and may even break its teeth and claws. In the final stage, the cat becomes progressively more PARALYSED from its rear quarters forwards, and this phase is called 'dumb' rabies. There is a characteristic change in the voice, which becomes husky as the result of effects on the throat muscles. Saliva drips from the mouth, and the cat may gradually lapse into COMA and death or die during the course of a CONVULSION. Death usually occurs within four or five days of the onset of symptoms.

In countries where rabies is endemic, including most of Europe, the virus persists in a variety of wild animals. These are an ever-present source of infection for domestic pets, which can be effectively protected only if all are vaccinated. Unfortunately, there are always some that slip through the net, and this is the reason why vaccination is not permitted in the UK because it is feared that it would lead to a relaxation in people's attitude to rabies. Vigilant quarantine and other regulations governing the movement of animals has so far kept the UK free of the disease. At present, there are calls for vaccination rather than quarantine of incoming pets to be given greater prominence.

radiography the DIAGNOSTIC TECHNIQUE of examining the body using X-rays. A radiograph is obtained, which can aid diagnosis and treatment of, e.g. DISLOCATIONS, FRACTURES and the location of TUMOURS or swallowed objects.

ranula a lump beneath the tongue that is usually caused by a blocked salivary gland duct.

rickets a malformation of the bones of young mammals caused by a deficiency of vitamin D. It is rarely seen in cats.

ringworm a highly infectious disease that attacks the hairs and outer layers of dead skin and is readily transmitted from one mammal to another and to people. Ringworm is a fungal infection, and the common causal fungus in cats is called *Microsporum canis*. Ringworm typically appears as circular, bare skin lesions with raised, dry, crusted edges. They are not always circular, however, and may appear as bare patches that gradually enlarge as the infection spreads. Young cats are most susceptible to ringworm because of their immature immune system, and the lesions are worse if there is a deficiency in vitamin A. Usually the lesions do not itch so scratching is not a particular problem.

A cat with a suspected ringworm infection must be examined and treated by a veterinary surgeon. It may be necessary to identify the fungus by examining hair samples under ultraviolet light. *Microsporum canis* emits a characteristic yellow-green fluorescence that is not given off by some other fungi that cause ringworm. Treatment has to be thorough, and because of the contagious nature of the infection, all pets and home surroundings should be included. It is preferable to burn all bedding and other items used by an infected cat although particular strong disinfectants can be used. The infected animal must be kept isolated and treated with tablets containing the anti-ringworm preparation Griseofulvin, while other fungicidal preparations are used directly on the lesions themselves. It may be necessary to continue treatment for some time as the infection can be quite resistant and persistent. Griseofulvin must not be given to a pregnant cat as it can cause developmental abnormalities in the foetuses.

People involved with an infected cat should take precautions, wear gloves, wash their hands and keep handling to a minimum. Medical attention should be sought if any member of the family develops a skin irritation. Always treat ringworm promptly before it has a chance to spread.

rodent ulcer *see* ULCER.

self-mutilation there are a number of circumstances in which self-mutilation, in the form of biting and scratching, can occur. It is generally provoked by extreme itching, and commonly occurs in cats as a result of the presence of EAR MITES or other external parasites (*see* PARASITES—External Parasites, page 140). Some hormonal disorders can cause severe itching, leading to self-mutilation, as can the viral disease PSEUDORABIES.

sedatives there are a number of circumstances in which it may be necessary to give a cat a sedative drug or tranquillizer, mainly those in which it is in pain or fearful and liable to bite and scratch or if it suffers from TRAVEL SICKNESS.

shock a serious physiological condition of acute circulatory failure in which the blood pressure in the arteries is too low to provide the normal blood, and hence oxygen supply, to the body. There are numerous different causes, and it is a life-threatening condition requiring emergency first aid and urgent veterinary treatment for the affected cat (*see* A-Z OF FIRST AID FOR CATS, page 238).

simulated illness it is not unknown for a cat to feign the symptoms of an illness or disorder from which it has recovered in order to regain the attention that it received at that time. This is generally not constant, and it is probably best to give the cat plenty of attention while it is not behaving in this way while ignoring it when it is.

stomach worms internal parasites that are flukes that occasionally infect cats in parts of the USA. They can cause VOMITING and loss of appetite.

strabismus 'crossed eyes', a condition that usually occurs only in excessively inbred pedigree cats such as some Siamese cats.

strained muscles strains and sprains are relatively uncommon in cats, compared to dogs, probably because of their great agility. Back and leg muscles may occasionally be involved as a result of an overambitious jump. Symptoms include pain or tenderness, which should resolve with rest. It is best to seek veterinary advice to confirm the diagnosis.

stress it is recognized that cats can suffer from stress, anxiety and insecurity, which usually manifest themselves in behavioural changes or physical symptoms such as VOMITING. Causes include a change in the home environment, such as the arrival of a new pet or baby, or being boarded in a cattery. Usually problems can be overcome by sympathetic treatment and removal of the cause if this is possible.

stud tail *see* SEXUAL BEHAVIOUR AND BREEDING—Male Cat, page 92.

sunburn rarely a problem in cats, but it may affect the ear tips of white cats in hot countries. Susceptible animals should be protected with sun cream and kept indoors during the hottest part of the day.

superfecundation *see* SEXUAL BEHAVIOUR AND BREEDING—Female Cat, page 94.

tail injuries the cat's tail is long, highly mobile and quite prone to accidental injury and damage. Injuries include FRACTURES, DISLOCATIONS, BITES, ABSCESSES and BLEEDING. As with any other type of injury, veterinary attention is needed and emergency FIRST AID may be required. Sometimes amputation of a severely damaged tail may be necessary.

tartar *see* GROOMING AND CARE—Care of Teeth, page 68.

temperature a cat's temperature is usually taken by gently inserting a thermometer into the rectum. The normal temperature is in the region of 38.5°C (101.5°F) but can rise much higher during the course of an illness or infection. A persistent rise or fall in temperature is a cause for concern, and the cat should be seen by a veterinary surgeon.

tetanus an infectious disease with the common name lockjaw, caused by the bacterium *Clostridium tetani*, which lives in the soil. It is extremely rare in cats.

thirst a cat should have access to clean drinking water at all times to satisfy its natural thirst and to replace water that has already been lost from the body. The only exception to this is if the cat has been VOMITING, when it is advisable to withhold both food and water for a time. An increased thirst can be a sign of an illness or infection, the cause of which should be investigated by a veterinary surgeon.

threadworms (*Strongyloides stercoralis*) uncommon internal parasites of cats that can cause COUGHING and DIARRHOEA.

toxoplasmosis an illness caused by a parasite protozoan microorganism called *Toxoplasma gondii*, which completes the sexual stage of its life cycle in cats, which are its final host. The organism passes out in the faeces of the cat, infected mice or birds. In all animals, once ingested, the parasites are carried in the bloodstream to other tissues and organs, lodging mainly in the muscles, lungs, brain, heart and eye. Here they may either form harmless cysts that remain dormant or proliferate rapidly by asexual reproduction, causing an acute attack of the symptoms of toxoplasmosis. These include a high temperature and a variety of other symptoms, depending upon the organ involved. In general, symptoms are mild and pass unnoticed, and they remain encysted. If the animal's immune system is compromised in any way, however, or if it becomes debilitated, the cysts may become active and replicate, causing a flare-up of symptoms. In cats, some parasites reproduce sexually in the digestive tract and produce infective cysts that pass out with the faeces.

The main danger occurs during pregnancy when the cysts become active and the parasites pass to developing foetuses. If *Toxoplasma* is contracted during pregnancy, the organism can be responsible for causing deformities, hydrocephalus, brain damage, mental retardation, blindness or even stillbirth in a human infant. People are infected by eating undercooked meat or through direct contact with infected cats and are especially at risk when handling litter trays. Pregnant women should avoid contact with litter trays, maintain a strict standard of hygiene and keep handling of a pet cat to a minimum. It is estimated that many people, cats and other animals worldwide have been exposed to *Toxoplasma* but never show signs of illness. If symptoms do occur in either animals or humans, drugs are available to treat them.

travel sickness cats occasionally suffer from travel sickness. The animal is usually quiet at first and then begins to retch and VOMIT. This is caused by disturbance of the organs of balance in the inner ear as a result of the motion of the vehicle. A cat that suffers from travel sickness should not be given anything to eat or drink prior to, or during, its journey. If necessary, a veterinary surgeon can supply a SEDATIVE tablet so that the cat will sleep during the journey.

trench mouth a bacterial disease that is common in cats and is similar to the trench fever that afflicted soldiers during World

War I. It causes a painful inflamed mouth and gums (GINGIVI-TIS), BAD BREATH and possibly ULCERATION. If untreated, the teeth may become loose and fall out, and the infection can even spread to the underlying bone in severe cases. Treatment with antibiotics will kill the infection, and the cat may need special feeding if it has lost condition.

tumour any abnormal swelling occurring in any part of the body consisting of an unusual growth of tissue, which may be malignant or benign. Tumours tend to be classified according to the tissue of which they are composed and produce varying symptoms according to their site within the body (*see also* CANCER).

ulcer a break on the skin surface or on a mucous membrane lining a body cavity that is inflamed, infected and slow to heal. Cats can develop ulcers as a result of various diseases and conditions. Sites include the tongue (ulcerative glossitis), mouth, nose and eye (ulcerative keratitis) as a result of FELINE RESPIRATORY DISEASE, and internal organs because of ingestion of poisonous substances such as aspirin (*see* POISONING).

A 'rodent' ulcer is a chronic, dry, ulcerated lesion that can develop on the upper lip of a cat. In order to stop it from spreading, it needs to be treated with certain drugs prescribed by a veterinary surgeon.

uraemia the condition in which there is excess urea (a metabolic by-product of protein) in the blood as a result of KIDNEY FAILURE. A cat with this condition is usually terminally ill.

vomeronasal organs (Jacobson's organs) a pair of small olfactory organs located near the roof of a cat's mouth that contain cells sensitive to chemical odours. These organs form part of the mechanism that gives the cat its keen sense of smell.

vomiting the reflex action whereby the stomach contents are expelled through the mouth because of the contraction of the diaphragm and abdominal wall muscles. Vomiting is caused by stimulus of the appropriate centre in the brain but the primary agent is usually a sensation from the stomach itself, such as an irritant or toxic substance or gastric disease. TRAVEL SICKNESS is another cause resulting from disturbance of the organs of balance in the inner ear.

Vomiting is common in cats because of a minor digestive upset or to eliminate a FUR BALL, and in this case there probably will be no other symptoms. Food should not be given for about eight hours, but a small quantity of water can be offered after two hours if this does not provoke more vomiting. Continue to give water every hour until the cat is no longer thirsty. When feeding is resumed, offer a small quantity of a bland food at first and then gradually increase the quantity to the normal amount. If vomiting resumes, is persistent or is accompanied by other symptoms, take the cat for veterinary examination and treatment.

weight loss unexplained weight loss in a cat is a cause for concern and evidence of some underlying disease or disorder that requires veterinary investigation.

wounds *see* A-Z OF FIRST AID FOR CATS, page 240.

A-Z of First Aid for Cats

The aim of first aid, in cats as in people, is to provide effective, on-the-spot treatment for an injury, illness or disorder when this is appropriate. The circumstances in which first aid are appropriate are:

1 When, without intervention, the cat is likely to experience greater suffering.

2 Its condition might deteriorate further.

3 It might die without immediate help.

In practice, it is not always obvious when these circumstances apply, and it can be difficult for an inexperienced person to know what to do. It is best, therefore, to carry out an immediate assessment based on common sense, provide treatment when it is judged to be needed and telephone and/or transport the cat to a veterinary surgeon.

First aid treatment varies from something as simple as keeping a cat still, warm and calm to giving ARTIFICIAL RESPIRATION because breathing has stopped. The following applies to simple measures that can be carried out by an inexperienced person, often in an emergency. Inevitably, there is some overlap with some of the conditions covered in the preceding section. To minimize the risk of either personal injury or further damage to the cat, the animal must be approached and handled properly. A seriously ill or injured cat is less likely to be able to resist your attentions but this is by no means always the case.

artificial respiration artificial respiration is needed whenever a cat has stopped breathing, and it may also be the case that the heart has ceased to beat. The heart's action pumps blood around the body, and the brain suffers irrevocable damage if it is deprived of oxygen for more than a few minutes. Artificial respiration may therefore be combined with heart massage in a technique known as CARDIOPULMONARY RESUSCITATION (CPR).

There are a number of circumstances that may cause breathing to cease, including anaphylactic shock, ASPHYXIA, DROWNING, ELECTROCUTION, accidental injuries, BLEEDING, CHOKING SHOCK and concussion. If breathing is shallow and slight it can be difficult to detect. One way of checking is to place your cheek near to the cat's mouth and nose to feel expired breath on your skin or hold a piece of fine tissue there which will move when the animal breathes out. Proceed only if you are sure that breathing has stopped.

First, hold the cat upside down by its thighs and swing it strongly from side to side about five times. This may be sufficient to restart breathing. If this fails, place the cat on its (uninjured) side (if applicable) with its head and neck extended forwards and any collar removed. The mouth and throat should be quickly checked for obstructions and the tongue pulled forwards. Ideally, the cat's head should be lower than its body, especially in cases of drowning. Both hands should then be placed over the ribs in the region of the chest and firm downward pressure exerted and then immediately released. The downwards pressure drives air out of the lungs, and these then expand and fill once more as the chest wall rises. Press sufficiently hard to depress the ribs but do not use excessive force. Repeat after five seconds and, following a few cycles, check to see if breathing has started and for the presence of a heartbeat—feel with your hand across the chest just behind the front legs. As long as the heartbeat continues, artificial respiration will ensure that vital oxygen is released into the blood. This technique is not effective, however, if the cat has a punctured lung or deep wound in the chest cavity when the MOUTH TO NOSE method must be used instead.

bleeding or **haemorrhage** external bleeding is dangerous only if a large blood vessel is involved, particularly if this is an artery, when the amount lost can quickly become life-threatening. An attempt must be made to stop profuse bleeding from a vein or artery by applying a pressure bandage. This is a thick pad of any suitable absorbent material, ideally the sterile, non-stick dressings that can be purchased from a chemist. In an emergency any clean material can be used—handkerchiefs, strips of towel, tea towel, cotton wool pads, etc. Hold the pad firmly on the site and secure it, ideally using a gauze or crepe bandage but a tie, scarf or strip of material can be used in an emergency. If it becomes soaked with blood, repeat without removing the first bandage but secure more tightly the second time.

The pressure exerted must be great enough to encourage clotting and the cessation of bleeding but not so tight as to cut off the blood circulation to other tissues. If it is clear that the pressure bandage is *not* working, then direct pressure on the artery

Control of severe bleeding.
Ask for assistance in restraining the cat and gently but firmly apply a thick pad of absorbent material over the site of the haemorrhage and bandage in place with a bandage or other suitable material.

supplying the wound can be attempted to stem the flow. The main pressure points are illustrated in the diagram. If serious arterial bleeding is occurring from a wound in the limb and this has not stopped with a pressure bandage, a tourniquet can alternatively be applied. A handkerchief, tie or strip of material is wrapped and tied tightly above the point of bleeding (nearest the body) and, if necessary, a pencil or other suitable instrument is slipped between the layers and rotated to exert greater pressure. A tourniquet should not be left in place for more than ten minutes, and this, and direct pressure on an artery, should only be used *as a last resort* to save the cat's life.

A cat's ears are quite liable to injury and tend to bleed profusely. If the flap of the ear is bleeding, a clean, absorbent pad should be placed on either side and pressure applied with the fingers for some minutes. With the pads still in place, the in-

Temporary control of serious haemorrhage.
Where there is very severe bleeding from the hind or front leg, the tail, head and neck, press with the fingers at the appropriate points to exert pressure on the artery supplying the area. This should be attempted only if the use of a pad and bandage cannot control the bleeding.

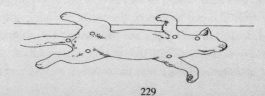

jured ear should be laid flat across the head and secured firmly with a crepe bandage, if one is available. This should be wrapped around the head and throat, taking care not to tighten it up too much as this may restrict the cat's breathing. The uninjured ear should be left free, and this helps to prevent the bandage from slipping. If bleeding is coming from within the ear, the opening should be plugged with a suitably sized clean pad before bandaging.

If bleeding is from a wound on the tongue or any part of the mouth, it is difficult to apply direct pressure with a conscious cat because of the risk of being bitten. The head should be kept low so that blood flows downwards and outwards to minimize the risk of choking. Depending upon the site of the wound, it may be possible to pinch the skin externally and apply pressure in that way.

If blood is coming from the nose no attempt should be made to cover the nostrils as, again, there is a risk of choking. A pad soaked in cold water and then wrung out should be placed over the bridge of the nose in an attempt to stop the bleeding. It may be the case, however, that the bleeding is caused by some internal injury, in which case this measure is not likely to help. Bleeding from the eye should be treated in a similar way. A clean pad, soaked in cold water and then wrung out, should be gently held over the eye while the cat is being restrained.

It is not uncommon for a cat to cut or break a claw, and this may bleed profusely. The wound should be covered with a clean dressing and the paw bandaged. No attempt should be made to remove the broken claw, and the cat should be taken to a veterinary surgeon.

Internal bleeding usually results from a severe blow to the body or head. It most commonly occurs as a result of a road traffic accident but may be caused by a fall from a height onto a hard surface. Internal bleeding is very serious as, unless it quickly stops, the cat is likely to pass into shock. In some cases, there may be some issue of blood from the mouth, nose and ears or it may be present in vomit, urine or faeces. The cat should be laid on its side with its head and neck extended, and a pillow or folded coat placed under the rear quarters and hind legs. It should be covered with a blanket and taken to a veterinary clinic without delay.

broken bones and **dislocations** (*see also* dislocation and fracture in A-Z OF ILLNESSES, pages 173, 189) these injuries, generally caused by road traffic accidents, are very painful, and it may be wise to restrain the cat by wrapping it in a coat or blanket. Approach the cat confidently and quietly, talking to it all the time. You may be able to take hold of the cat by the scruff of the neck with one hand, using the other to support its body. Alternatively, you may need to try to drop a coat over the cat and tuck it round quickly before lifting the animal.

back spinal fractures are very serious and may cause paralysis of the area of the body below the injury. Carefully slide the cat onto a firm flat surface such as a large piece of wood. Place one hand under the shoulders and the other beneath the hips and do not move the spine as this may cause further damage.

limbs try to persuade the cat to lie in a bed, box or basket with the injured limb uppermost. A clean, folded towel should be gently pulled beneath the injured leg to provide support. If a broken bone is protruding through the skin, this should be covered with another clean towel or pad.

ribs if fractured or dislocated ribs are suspected, wrap a towel completely around the body between the front and hind limbs to provide some support. Do not wrap too tightly in case this interferes with breathing. Try to keep the cat lying down in its bed or basket.

tail usually, there is no need to bandage this unless there is severe bleeding.

In all cases, do not give the cat anything to eat or drink and take it immediately to a veterinary clinic. It is likely to be given a general anaesthetic so that the injury can be dealt with. Always observe the cat for signs of SHOCK.

burns and **scalds** burns and scalds produce similar symptoms, but the former are caused by dry heat and the latter by moist heat. Burns may also be caused by ELECTRIC SHOCK and caustic chemicals (*see* poisoning in A-Z OF ILLNESSES, page 207). Cats are particularly at risk in kitchens through knocking over scalding liquids or burning their paws on hot plates.

Formerly burns were classified by 'degrees' but they are now described either as 'superficial', where sufficient tissue remains to ensure regrowth, or 'deep'. With deep burns, all the affected layers of skin are destroyed and underlying tissues are exposed. Healing is prolonged and difficult, and there is usually considerable scarring, pain and disfigurement. With all burns, but particularly with deep ones, the main risk is the development of SHOCK and infection. Sometimes, especially in cats with abundant fur, the extent of the damage is not immediately apparent, and blisters and weeping wounds may appear some time later. First aid treatment consists of soaking the area with cold water for about ten or fifteen minutes. Cold water can be poured over the burn or a shower attachment may be used. If the skin is intact, a clean, nonstick dressing and bandage can be placed over the area, and a veterinary surgeon should be contacted for further advice. If the skin is broken, the wound should ideally be covered with a clean, sterile, nonstick medical dressing that is bandaged into place. In an emergency, however, any clean covering may be used, such as a tea towel or pillow case, and the cat must be taken immediately to a veterinary clinic. If burns are either deep or extensive, the outlook is usually poor, and a veterinary surgeon may advise euthanasia to avoid further suffering.

cardiopulmonary resuscitation (CPR) an emergency procedure combining MOUTH TO NOSE ARTIFICIAL RESPIRATION with cardiac massage. It is used as a last resort to save the life of a cat that has ceased to breathe and has no heartbeat. To check for breathing, place your cheek next to the cat's nose and mouth to feel for breath or place a tissue there to see if it moves with expired air. To check for a heartbeat, place a hand around the chest just behind the front limbs with fingers and thumb on either side. If breathing and heartbeat are absent, lay the unconscious cat on its side and open its mouth. Pull the tongue forward and check for and remove any debris that is present. Push the tongue back and close the mouth, placing one hand around the nose and jaws. Place your mouth completely over the cat's nose and blow firmly so that the lungs inflate and the rib cage rises. Remove your mouth and allow the lungs to deflate and the rib cage to fall. Continue for ten seconds (about four or five blows) and then carry out heart massage. Place one hand against the cat's back and the other around the rib cage just behind the front legs with fingers and thumb on either side. Compress the rib cage with a forwards motion and continue for fifteen seconds. Check for a return of heartbeat and continue as necessary. As long as the heart is beating, mouth to nose resuscitation will provide the cat with sufficient oxygen to maintain life. Pause after every two inflations to see if the cat begins to breathe on its own. It should be appreciated that it is often not possible for a cat in this condition to survive in spite of your best efforts at revival.

choking violent coughing and inability to breathe caused by an obstruction of the windpipe by an object that the cat has picked up in its mouth. Fortunately, this is less of a problem in cats than in dogs, but may occur as a result of a trapped piece of food (usually a bone) or fragment of a chewed toy. In dealing with a conscious choking cat, the main problem is that the animal is extremely frightened and agitated. It helps if two people are available, one to restrain the cat. If not, wrap the cat completely in a towel, leaving only its head free. Hold the cat on a table against your body with one arm, using the same hand to grasp the head and face on each side of the upper jaw. Raise the head to open the mouth and if you can see the object and it is not too far back, then attempt to loosen and dislodge it with a blunt instrument, tweezers or a fine pair of pliers.

It is essential to work quickly, and there is a risk of pushing the object further down. Take care not to remove an object that appears to be attached to string or thread as this may be attached to an object that is in the stomach.

If this fails, hold the cat upside down by its thighs and swing

235

choking

First aid for a choking cat.

Open the mouth   *Pry out the object*

it from side to side and shake it lightly. This may dislodge the
object, which it is to be hoped will fall out of the mouth. If the
cat is still choking or is unconscious, place it on its side on a
table. Place one hand on its back and the other on the abdomen
just behind the rib cage. Squeeze downwards and forwards

First aid for a choking cat—shake the cat.

*Hold the cat's thighs firmly and
then gently shake and swing it*

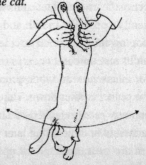

firmly in a rapid movement. This expels a burst of air from the lungs and hopefully dislodges the object.

With all these procedures, it is necessary to be sure that the dislodged object is removed from the cat's mouth. If the cat does not begin to breathe spontaneously, it may be necessary to give artificial respiration or CARDIOPULMONARY RESUSCITATION. In all cases, take the cat for veterinary examination as it may have sustained injuries to its throat and require further treatment.

dislocations *see* BROKEN BONES.

drowning most cats dislike open water and do not venture too near so drowning incidents are less common than with dogs. If a cat has been pulled out of the water and has ceased to breathe, its lungs will be filled with water. First wipe the cat's nose and mouth, both inside and out, to clear them of any weed or other debris. Then hold the cat upside down by its thighs and shake it gently up and down so that the lungs empty. Swing the cat from side to side to try to restart breathing. If this fails, place the cat on its side with its head lower than the rest of its body. Check for a heartbeat and then proceed with ARTIFICIAL RESPIRATION or CARDIOPULMONARY RESUSCITATION as required. Even if the cat apparently recovers, there is a real risk of complications, particularly shock, developing later so always take the animal for veterinary treatment.

electrocution and **electric shock** electric shock or electrocution usually occur as a result of a kitten chewing through the cable of a household appliance. Rarely, a cat may wander onto a live electric railway line or be struck by lightning. Of course, in many cases the electric shock is instantly fatal and there may also be severe BURNS. The first priority is to isolate the cat from the power source—unless this can be safely accomplished, no attempt should be made at rescue. If this can be achieved, check for heartbeat and breathing and give ARTIFICIAL RESPIRATION and CARDIOPULMONARY RESUSCITATION as appropriate. If this is successful, take the cat immediately to a veterinary surgeon as there is a risk of further complications, especially the development of SHOCK.

haemorrhage *see* BLEEDING.

heart massage *see* CARDIOPULMONARY RESUSCITATION.

mouth-to-nose resuscitation a type of artificial respiration that may be given if a cat has ceased to breathe. The technique is described under CARDIOPULMONARY RESUSCITATION. This method is the best one to use if a cat has any form of deep chest wound where there is reason to suspect that a lung is pierced or damaged. Frothy blood, i.e. mixed with air, coming from the nose or mouth or appearing at the wound surface is one indication of such damage.

shock physiological shock is a condition of acute circulatory failure in which the arterial blood pressure is too low to provide the normal blood and oxygen supply to the body. In cats, shock can arise following any illness, injury, accident or trauma. It can occur quite soon after a particular incident or arise much later, following an apparent recovery. It is a serious and potentially life-threatening condition and must be dealt with immediately should any signs occur.

One important early indication of shock is pallor of the gums. Normally, the gums should be definitely pink, and if a portion is pinched between a finger and thumb, the blood (and hence the colour) should return immediately. In early shock, the colour is very pale and is slow in returning when the gum is pinched. Other indications include rapid breathing (35 to 40 breaths per minute) and heartbeat rate (in excess of 120 beats per minute), restlessness or apathy and vomiting. Later the breathing becomes slow and slight and the heartbeat is irregular, the cat slips into unconsciousness and has white- or blue-tinged gums and a lowered body temperature. It may shiver and the paws are very cold. First aid treatment consists of lying the cat down on its side and stretching the head and neck forwards. Cushions, folded blankets or whatever is available should be used to raise the hindquarters so that blood flows forwards. ARTIFICIAL RESPIRATION or CARDIOPULMONARY RESUSCITATION may be needed, and the cat should be covered with a blanket to keep it warm. Immediate emergency veterinary treatment is needed, and the cat is likely to require close monitoring and intensive care.

wounds the severity of a wound varies from serious and life-threatening to relatively minor. All carry the risk of infection and therefore need to be thoroughly cleaned. If there is profuse BLEEDING this should be dealt with first. A minor wound can be thoroughly washed with plenty of warm water containing an antiseptic solution, and a clean dressing and bandage can then be applied. If a wound is obviously deep or severe, however, it is best not to waste time trying to deal with it at home but to cover it with clean material and get immediate veterinary assistance.

Any wound, including one with stitches following an operation, can become infected. Signs of infection include heat, swelling, pain and a discharge containing pus. If this occurs, the cat should be taken to a veterinary surgeon for treatment. It will probably require antibiotic drugs and may need sedatives or a general ANAESTHETIC so that the wound can be thoroughly cleaned and dressed.